Global Engineering Project Managment

Global Engineering Project Managment

M. Kemal Atesmen

CRC Press
Taylor & Francis Group
Boca Raton   London   New York

CRC Press is an imprint of the
Taylor & Francis Group, an **informa** business

AN AUERBACH BOOK

Auerbach Publications
Taylor & Francis Group
6000 Broken Sound Parkway NW, Suite 300
Boca Raton, FL 33487-2742

Library of Congress Cataloging-in-Publication Data

Atesmen, M. Kemal.
    Global engineering project management / M. Kemal Atesmen.
        p. cm.
    Includes bibliographical references and index.
    ISBN 978-1-4200-7393-5 (alk. paper)
        1. Project management. 2. Engineering--International cooperation. 3.
International business enterprises--Management. I. Title.

T56.8.A84 2008
658.4'04--dc22   2007049113

Visit the Taylor & Francis Web site at
http://www.taylorandfrancis.com

and the Auerbach Web site at
http://www.auerbach-publications.com

Contents

Preface

This book covers some of the errors that were made, issues that came up, difficulties that were encountered, and lessons that were learned while managing international engineering projects. All the examples and cases were taken from my engineering notebooks that covered project issues, lessons learned lists, project meeting minutes, action items lists, videoconference and teleconference notes, etc.

Many young engineers all over the world receive some level of engineering education, then are thrown into a professional career without proper mentoring and without organized training for further development. This gap between academics and practice causes errors, project delays, and bottom line losses for industries. When you add the variances in international standards, specifications, measurement units, cultures, politics, etc., the gap between academics and practice widens. This book tries to narrow this gap for young engineers who are destined for international project management.

In today's global economy, I have not encountered a project that does not have an international component. Even U.S.-based projects can have international subcontractors, international competition, international patent infringements, etc. There have been many books written on project management principles and practices, but none of them covers the international aspects of engineering project management.

The book is divided into six chapters that take the reader through an international engineering project from inception to completion.

Chapter 1 expands on the characteristics of an engineering project and details the factors that come into the picture when a project becomes international.

Chapter 2 details the responsibilities of an engineering project manager when the project expands into the international arena.

Chapter 3 provides tips for writing technical proposals for international bids.

Chapter 4 details the planning and start-up phase of an international engineering project.

Chapter 5 provides the focal points in executing an international engineering project.

Chapter 6 details the tasks that have to be completed in closing out an international engineering project.

A checklist is provided at the end of each chapter to guide the international engineering project manager through that particular phase of the project.

Because no two engineering project managers manage his or her project the same way, this book should be taken as a guide in international engineering project management. Examples and cases provided here should be stepping stones for individual international engineering project management experience and for improving individual international engineering project management techniques.

M. Kemal Atesmen
Santa Barbara, California

Acknowledgments

Over 33 years of engineering project management in the international arena covering automotive, computer, data communication, and offshore oil industries were accomplished by exceptional support from my wife, Zeynep, and my son, Omer. Some years I was away from home more than six months out of a year.

I would like to dedicate this book to all the project team members with whom I had the pleasure of working over the years, who did the hard work with enthusiasm, and who kept coming back to work along with me on a project team without any reservations.

M. Kemal Atesmen
Santa Barbara, California

Introduction

We live in a world of global economy. In this day and age, it is hard to encounter an engineering project that does not deal with multiple countries and cultures. This book covers the challenges that an international engineering project manager encounters during the life of an international project and provides real cases to expand on these challenges. Each chapter ends with a summary checklist to provide the project manager with a list of reminders.

Chapter 1 deals with the factors that characterize an international engineering project. These factors range from technologies, virtual teams, traditions, economies, and politics to legal issues.

Chapter 2 details the responsibilities of an international engineering project manager in his worldwide environment. These responsibilities cover international team(s) leadership, motivation, filtering, being an ambassador, communications, time management, and supervising the project honeymoon period.

Most engineering project managers get involved at the technical proposal write-up phase of an international project. Chapter 3 provides pointers and tips about how to prepare a technical proposal. It also details the ways to a winning project bidding process.

When an international project is given the green light, planning the project takes an enormous amount of effort from the project manager. Chapter 4 details this initial phase of an international project. Selecting the domestic and international team members, creating a summary of project specifications and standards, creating the work breakdown structure, generating the initial project schedule, setting up the project information management system, having the project kickoff meetings, and setting up project schedule and cost performance indices are part of the planning phase, namely the foundation of the project.

Chapter 5 details the execution phase of an international engineering project. The chapter starts with management of international teams, customers, subcontractors, upper managements, and regulatory agencies. Afterward, the chapter covers the issues that an international engineering project manager will more than likely encounter and have to control during the execution of an international project. These include surprises, errors, listening, practical solutions, whatever-it-takes, meetings, status reports, confidentiality and intellectual property requirements, risk management, fire fighting, adapting to change, controlling the project, training, and time-off.

Chapter 6 details the tasks that an international engineering project manager has to complete while closing out a project. Most international engineering projects do not have a clean-cut closure, the scope changes or the overall project delays, etc. The tasks that are outlined in Chapter 6 have to be fitted to the phase-out mode of the project. Final project status reports, domestic and international team member performance evaluations, lessons learned during the project execution, and customers' project report cards are some of the project closure tasks that an international engineering project manager has to perform before going on to new endeavors.

About the Author

M. Kemal Atesmen completed all of his degrees in mechanical engineering. He earned his B.Sc. from Case Western Reserve University, Cleveland, Ohio, M.Sc. from Stanford University, Stanford, California, and Ph.D. from Colorado State University in Fort Collins. He is a life member of the American Society of Mechanical Engineers. He initially pursued academic and industrial careers in parallel and became an associate professor in mechanical engineering before dedicating his professional life to international engineering project management and engineering management for 33 years. He helped many young engineers in the international arena to bridge the gap between college and professional life in automotive, computer component, data communication, and offshore oil industries.

Chapter 1

What Is an International Engineering Project?

A typical international engineering project to design, build, test, deliver, and install a system starts with a set of specifications written in French; a budget in Euros; a schedule that covers all the time zones and holidays of several different countries; subsystems designed, built, and tested at several countries around the world, integrated into a system designed, built, and tested in the United States; and deliverables that end up in Russia.

In just-in-time volume production side, an international engineering project can go like this. Designing, prototyping, and qualification of computer disk drive magnetic heads are accomplished in the United States. Wafers for the magnetic heads are also manufactured in the United States. Wafers are sent to Malaysia and manufactured into subassemblies. Subassemblies are sent from Malaysia to South Korea and built into assemblies. Final disk drive head assemblies are sent from South Korea to Japan to go into a customer's fully automated disk drive assembly.

In general, an international project team is formed in order to perform the needed engineering tasks, prepare the deliverables, and satisfy the customer. However, there are quite a number of challenges in managing an international engineering project that are not normally encountered in a domestic engineering project. These challenges can cover a wide range of technological, virtual team environment, traditional, economic, political, legal, and other factors.

Technological Factors

Technological factors that affect an international project can be broken down into applicable technical specifications and standards, training, infrastructure, and application tools.

In an international engineering project, technical specifications and standards that apply may not be the same as the ones we are used to in the United States. There can be differences in electrical codes, safety standards, welding standards, tolerancing and dimensioning standards, regulatory agency design, and test certification rules and procedures, and so forth. Units used in the project can be the International System of Units (SI), English units, or a combination. In international projects, there will also be differences in electrical power requirements, environmental criteria, spare parts requirements, material specifications, and in many other areas.

Before taking on an international project, all the ambiguous items in the specifications and standards must be clarified. If the project is going to run in English, then all the project specifications should be translated into English by a qualified translator. If the project team is not familiar with the applicable standards, propose to the customer to specify the U.S. standards, or a combination of U.S. standards and the extra requirements above and beyond the U.S. standards. Extra requirements above and beyond the U.S. standards should be clearly identified and outlined to the team members.

Sometimes a combination of standards can be confusing and can cause disputes and conflicts. For example, an equipment system was designed and built in the United States for a Norwegian customer. In their specifications, the Norwegians required a regulatory agency design certification and test witnessing by Det Norske Veritas (DNV) using the American Bureau of Shipping (ABS) rules. There are subtle differences between the DNV and ABS design rules, such as allowable design stress levels, material property requirements, and others. Also, the DNV design reviewers and inspectors are not trained in the details of the ABS rules. Applying such a combination of international standards can be costly and can bring extra and unnecessary burden to the project.

Units for the project have to be clearly understood. In several cases, you might have to use dual units. For example, if the customer is in the United States and the design is performed there, but the components are built in South Korea, then both SI and English units have to be put on all the documents. This duality in units causes errors and increases the time for document checking. Another example is gauge units. For unit of pressure on a pressure gauge, customers could specify "bar," "atm," "mPa," or "psi."

In international engineering projects, simple things such as thread callouts, port and tube/hose connection callouts, or material callouts might be very confusing and require extensive retraining. For example, you might be used to UN/UNF thread callouts in the United States, but you might have to switch to metric ones. Your port and tube fittings might have been National Pipe Thread Fuel (NPTF) or straight thread o-ring (SAE) callouts, but the international project might require British Standard Pipe Parallel (BSPP) or metric straight-thread o-ring ones. Even the lubricants you call out in your maintenance manual might not be available in the country you are dealing with, and you might have to investigate and find equivalent replacement lubricants.

Your customer's qualified subcontractor's list defines the products you can use in the project, as all equipment components must come from the customer's approved subcontractor's list. There might also be a list of subcontractors proposed by your company during contract negotiations and approved by the customer. There will also be a list of approved countries for the origin of materials that can be used in the project. For example, steels from several third-world countries are not approved for usage in some projects because of inconsistency in their quality. Some materials originating from some countries might require an independent third-party testing laboratory certification before they can be used in the project. These kinds of unusual material requirements will add extra time and cost to the project.

Another technological factor that requires careful and detailed planning is training. Some of the international team members might not be as advanced in the technology arena that you are dealing with. International engineers mostly have theoretical training at their universities and miss the practical and application portion of the technology. Training of virtual project-team members is a challenge in itself. Training teams might have to be sent to the international project sites, which adds more time and cost to the project.

For example, training an international team that is going to operate and maintain an automated manufacturing module designed and built in the United States might take months. There might be a continuous support team from the United States on location, helping and advising the operation and maintenance team on the automated module. Just installing a complicated piece of equipment or a system in a foreign country and leaving it to the local teams for operation and maintenance after a short training may be fine due to cost and trainer availability restraints, but it will destine the project to a tragic fate. Undertraining for installation, maintenance, and operation will cause numerous warranty issues and will cost your company much more in the long run.

Training virtual team member engineers for leading-edge technologies will take more effort and time. Sometimes it might be feasible to send a technology expert to train the team members at the foreign site, and sometimes it is best to bring several virtual team members to the United States for a considerable duration and teach them the leading-edge technology at the home base.

Lack of infrastructure in the international project site can cause enormous stress and delays to a project. If you are planning to build a plant with a clean room in a country with continuous power outages and voltage fluctuations, you might need a noninterruptible power supply system to control temperature and humidity of the clean room. There might be more stringent filtering requirements for clean water and compressed air. On the nontechnical side, the plant infrastructure might require living quarters, praying sites, and security for the employees.

Another critical area is application tools. The international project site should have design, test, calibration, maintenance, and communication tools compatible with your U.S. base. If your customer is international, then you have to have design and communication tools compatible with your customer's. Design tools have to be at the same revision level. Test and calibration equipment and maintenance tools have to be of the same type and quality. A system that is built to unified national thread standards and sent over to a foreign country that is on a metric system can cause grief if several unified thread tool sets do not accompany the system. Communication tools have to be able to talk to each other, should be reliable, and should have backups.

Virtual Team Environment Factors

International project teams are very challenging to manage. A portion of the team might reside, say, in Malaysia. Time differences, lack of detailed communication, and lack of close monitoring and brainstorming can all increase the risk factor. Cultural and language differences also increase the risk factor in project performance. Remote controlling an international project is the most difficult job for an engineering project manager. You should do all you can to minimize this remoteness. Regular trips by the international team members to the United States or vice versa, training of international team members in the United States or vice versa, and tying in of the international team members during team meetings by videoconferencing are all a must. Of course, these extra costs and time losses have to be factored into the project plan.

To manage an international engineering project in a virtual environment starts with a good and dedicated project team at home and at the international project sites. Choosing the right team members and the international project sites team leaders are crucial to the success of a project in a virtual environment. Everyone in the team should work to the same project objectives with harmony and respect for the project manager. The project manager's challenge is to make the project objectives clear, bring harmony to the virtual teams, and gain everyone's respect at the planning and execution phases of the project. Initial face-to-face meetings, and assigning clear tasks, task completion dates, and clear project milestones and specifications go a long way in a successful international project.

Language barriers and a lot of head nods during face-to-face meetings or videoconferences should give the project manager an uneasy feeling. A sure way to clear the air is to ask your international team members to put their task objectives, action items, and action item completion dates in writing and e-mail them to you. Similar situations arise in customer meetings. A Japanese customer might nod his head meaning that he hears you, but may not agree with you. Again, putting the customer meeting's action items, their completion dates, all the agreed issues, and all the disputed issues in writing is a must. These written meeting minutes should be signed off both by you and the customer's project manager, and should be document controlled properly. In some cases, you might need a full-time technical translator on your team.

Traditional Factors

A country's traditional factors also affect an international project immensely. Working hours and attitudes can be quite different in Japan than in Malaysia. A Japanese engineer will not leave work before his or her supervisor leaves. In Japan, a project manager can encounter many 12-hour meetings going into midnight, and engineers wearing the same clothes two or three days in a row and dozing in their offices. Work traditions change from country to country and by time. Latitude and work attitude correlation have been seen in many countries. You as the project manager cannot change these habits; You have to live with them and adjust your project accordingly. Greetings, handshakes, lunches, business dinners, visiting someone's house, gifts, and taking shoes off when entering a house have a different approach in every culture. As an international engineering project manager, you have to learn and respect the traditions of the culture you are dealing with. A simple "thank you" in the native language, i.e., "domo arigato" in Japanese or "kamsahamnita" in Korean, goes a long way. At the end of a meeting in Japan, action items are written on the board with the names of owners and due dates. Once, at the end of a meeting, a project manager started the action items list with writing "action items" in Japanese Kanji characters on the board, and all his Japanese colleagues dropped from their seats and had a good laugh after a very long meeting.

Eating lunch with your colleagues and workers at the plant cafeteria instead of going out to an outside restaurant helps to bring unity and harmony to an international project team. In all projects domestic or international, the customer looks at the quality and timeliness of the deliverables. For an international customer, cultural and language differences make the relationship more delicate. At the top of the list are the peoples' names. Pronounce them correctly. If you have known your counterpart for a while, inquire about his family and his hobbies. When you visit a customer in Japan, you have to know how to sit around a conference table, how to exchange greetings, how to exchange small gifts, and when to talk during the meeting. Japanese customers put a lot of emphasis on the details of action items and on timely response to them.

It might be more difficult to learn who the decision makers are or what the pecking order is for an international customer. Also, it might be difficult to differentiate between technical, purchasing, and finance decision loops of an international customer.

Economic Factors

Economic factors of a country you are dealing with will affect your project, too. A customer's project manager in a third-world country might be making a salary a third of yours. A Japanese engineer can be living in a 1000 square foot home with his wife and three children. This engineer might be an avid golfer, but he cannot play at a regular 18-hole golf course because the fees are outrageous. Salary discussions and bragging about lifestyles can be very demoralizing in an international team environment. Simple things as staying in a normally rated hotel instead of a five-star one and going back and forth to work with the company van instead of a private chauffeured car might go a long way.

A third-world country project manager might ask you to include two extra laptops to the project equipment shipments. These kinds of sensitive requests should be discussed with your superiors, business people, and legal people before a final decision is made.

When you are a lone ranger in a foreign country to discuss only technical issues about the project with your customer, legal and business issues will come up. Comments and decisions made under pressure during the meeting regarding these nontechnical issues might put an engineering project manager in hot water. The best way to remedy the situation is to take notes and action items to be responded to by the appropriate people at your home base.

Political Factors

Political factors also affect an international project. World political alliances and tensions, historical animosities between nations, embargos, etc., can definitely dampen the progress of an international project. During operation Desert Storm (the first Iraq War), it was indeed very eerie feeling while traveling to Malaysia. All the international flights were empty and no carry-ons were allowed, not even a briefcase. Malaysia was generally pro-Saddam. You had to register your whereabouts in Malaysia with the U.S. Consulate and keep a low profile. You had to avoid discussing sensitive issues regarding the war. Some countries do not allow in their systems equipment made in Taiwan or in Israel. Some countries such as Korea and Japan, and Greece and Turkey, have historical animosities that are sensitive even to this day, ever-expanding global economy. The United States has in effect embargos to certain countries at certain times, and you might have to get special permits for shipment of high-technology equipment to certain countries.

Every team member traveling internationally should have a passport valid for at least six months beyond the duration of the project. The passports should have enough blank pages for visas. Another area of attention is the visas and work permits required for a country and the time to obtain them. All these intricate political factors can affect an international project's progress.

Legal Factors

Legal factors can hamper a project due to patent infringement issues, specification nonconformance issues, nonperformance issues, and project delays. If a course correction is not made in a timely fashion and the issue goes to lawyers, the results might hurt your customer and your company, and give you an incurable black eye in your industry. As a project manager, it is imperative for you to know all the milestones, deliverables and deliverable requirements, technical specifications, and change orders that govern the project agreement. Every document involving the project agreement should be controlled with revision levels.

In the event of any dispute between your customer and your company related to your project, a controlled and up-to-date project-related document set might save you a lot of grief. Most international project arbitrations are settled in the country of origin for the project, and the arbitration language might not be in English.

Other Factors

Project schedules are dynamic guides for an international project team. Before starting an international project, settle on the type of calendar to be used during the project. Will the project follow the international weekly calendar, your company's fiscal-accounting calendar, or some other calendar? When you present the project schedules, say, in Microsoft (MS) Project, will your customer be able to open the MS Project file? You might have to create your schedules in MS Project but transmit them as Acrobat PDF files. Do you know your international customer's weekend days, holidays, and plant closure dates? Have you included these special dates into the project schedule? In the project correspondence, are you going to use day/month/year or month/day/year for dates?

Other important drivers in an international project are the milestones. The milestones, their dates, the deliverables, payment procedures, and letters of credit have to be crystal clear. When you say you are going to ship on a certain day, do you mean according to Pacific Standard Time (PST) or according to Greenwich Mean Time (GMT)? If you are going to electronically submit a file to a customer in Germany on May 15, 2007, you had better put that deliverable on your project schedule to be sent on May 14, 2007, from California.

Shipping of components, finished products, spares, or other items in an international project need a lot of planning. Shipping costs and durations, customs clearance costs and durations, and letter-of-credit clearance costs and durations must all be accounted for in project costing, scheduling, and risk management. Shipment and delivery of finished products to a customer's facility in South Korea no later than May 1, 2007, will have quite different logistics for CIF (cost, insurance, freight) Pusan than for ex-works shipping requirements.

To upper management, budget is the most crucial of all the drivers in a project. You have to know the type of contract you will be working under. Do you know the currency of the bid? Is the contract in U.S. dollars or in Euros or in some other currency? Will the foreign currency parity fluctuations affect the project budget? If the project is a fixed-price contract, is there some contingency? Are there any liquidated damages for the delays? Everyone on the team should know the effects of liquidated damages to the company. Are there any early delivery rewards? Everyone should also know the effects of early delivery rewards, and should know the payment milestones and the affects of these payments on the company's cash flow.

Sometimes a new project might be a subsystem of a larger international project. In that case, it will be good to know if your project is on the critical path of the overall project. It will be also good to know if there is any slack time for your subproject in the overall project plan, and so you can negotiate some delay in delivery if it is needed. It is always a good idea to keep up to date regarding the status of the overall project, namely, always know the big picture. Another subsystem might be delaying the overall project, and that might give you a little breathing room. On the other side of the coin, time-to-market pressures might require your customer to ask you to expedite your deliverables by working overtime. It is always good to have a feel about the events that are affecting your international project at the customers' end.

Deliverables schedule, testing, and acceptance criteria must all be understood. Do you know the delivery terms for the equipment and for the documentation? Shipping conditions, final inspection release certificates, and technical passports, which all affect deliverables, must be crystal clear. Are equipment packaging requirements all clear? Are deliverable documents to be submitted in dual language? Are deliverable documents in a dual-unit system? What is the file format of the deliverable documents? For your design drawings, are you at the same AutoCad revision level as your customer? Can your customer use your solid-modeling files and incorporate them into their system design?

It takes a lot more preparation and detailed organizing when an international customer visits your facilities in the United States. Obtaining U.S. visas for them, providing driving accommodations in the United States, or setting up non-work-related side trips to shopping or to Disneyland all require extensive planning. You have to be cognizant of their culinary preferences and their jet-lag conditions.

There may also be times when your customer is in a bind. For example, let us say that they forgot to include a gauge into their specification and they ask you to include this extra gauge into the project without any extra cost or delay. As the engineering project manager, you should be able to offer small gestures to them without scope changes, contract amendments, etc., that might add more cost to both companies. Such gestures will give you brownie points in the customer's eyes. You might use these brownie points later when you are in a bind and need to ask the customer a favor.

Sometimes the customer changes its project manager in the middle of the project. You should bring the new project manager to the United States and get him or her up to speed on the project as a full team member. If the customer's project manager, or other engineers who are related to the project, are behind in the technology that you are working on, you should train them at their facility or at your facility in the United States and bring their technical level to an acceptable one without giving up all your intellectual property aces.

Also, in an international project it is good to know who your company's competitors are. Who were the bidders to your project? Why did they lose? Why did your company win? What are your company's strengths and weaknesses? How can you improve your company's performance in this project so that you can get more follow-on projects. It is always advisable to have a good rapport with your competitors' engineering managers and to know their strengths and weaknesses.

In summary, in comparison to a domestic engineering project, an international engineering project is more complex and more dynamic, has a lot more variables covering technical and nontechnical factors, requires more detailed planning with more unknowns or rough estimates, requires more precise time and communication management, and calls for fast-responding risk management.

In the following chapters, we will examine these areas in more detail, and present real cases and practical solutions and techniques to meet the project management challenges in international engineering projects.

Checklist for Chapter 1

Technological Factors

- Translate all project specifications into English.
- Clarify all applicable international standards for the project.
- Know all the required regulatory agency design and test-certification rules and procedures.
- Schedule to train your team members locally and internationally with the new applicable specifications and standards.
- Do you know in detail the infrastructure of the international project site that affects your project, power supply issues, humidity and temperature control issues, water supply issues, living quarters, security, etc.?
- Are the issues related to deficiencies in infrastructure included into the project specifications and deliverables?
- Agree on units to be used in the project.
- Agree on thread callout, material callouts, etc., to be used in the project.
- Agree on the approved subcontractors list.
- Do you know all the application tools requirements for the international project sites, i.e., compatible design tools, test tools, calibration tools, maintenance tools, communication tools, etc.?

Virtual Team Environment Factors

- Agree on the calendar to be used during the project.
- Have you chosen the right project leader for the international project site?
- Have you chosen the team members for the international project site?
- Have you met with the offshore team members face to face? Do you know each one's background and technological strengths and weaknesses?
- What are the language barriers? Do you need translators?
- Have you agreed with every offshore team member on his or her training requirements and schedules? Have you informed his or her supervisor about these requirements?
- Have you set clear communication procedures, i.e., set time for videoconferences, teleconferences, e-mail reports, etc., with the international sites?
- Have you decided on the international trips that are required during the project and clearly explained them to your offshore teams?
- Is every international team member of your team clear on project objectives?
- Has every international team member clearly assigned tasks and task completion dates?
- Is every international team member clear on project milestones, i.e., design review meetings, customer visits, qualification requirements, regulatory agency requirements, etc.?
- Is every international team member clear on applicable project specifications and standards?

Traditional Factors

- Do you know the working hours of your international partners?
- Do you know the work habits and attitudes of your international partners?
- Are you cognizant of all the do's and don'ts of the cultures you are dealing with?
- Have you scheduled to train your project team members in the United States with the do's and don'ts of the cultures you are dealing with?
- Do you know how to pronounce the names of the people you are dealing with in the international arena?
- Do you know the personnel structure of your international customer?
- Do you know the responsibilities of each player from your customer's team?

Economic Factors

- Do you have an understanding of the economic factors of the countries you are dealing with?

- Have you scheduled to train your project team members in the United States with the economic factors of the countries you are dealing with?
- Have you come up with a plan as to how to deal with your international customer's unusual requests above and beyond the contract deliverables?
- Do you have a plan as to how to deal with nontechnical issues that will come up during your international visits?

Political Factors

- Do you know the history of the countries that you are dealing with?
- What are their political alliances and who are their political enemies?
- Have you scheduled to train your project team members in the United States with the political factors of the countries you are dealing with?
- Do you know the visa and work permit requirements for the countries you are dealing with?

Legal Factors

- Do you know all the significant portions of your project agreement covering the milestones, deliverables, deliverable requirements, and change-order procedures?
- In the event a conflict occurs between various specifications and standards, do you know how to deal with it?
- Do you have a good procedure of controlling all the documents related to the project that can be used in case of a legal conflict?
- Do you know where and in which language the project arbitrations will be settled?

Other Factors

- What type of calendar will be used during the project?
- Does your customer and your other international project sites have the same scheduling software and revision level?
- Have you included the weekend days, holidays, and plant closure days of your international partners?
- Do you know the type of your project contract, i.e., fixed price, scoped time and material, unscoped time and material, etc.?
- Do you know your project currency?
- Is there any contingency in the project budget?
- Are there any liquidated damages?
- Are there any early delivery rewards?

- Is your project on the critical path of a parent project?
- What are the time zone differences with major players in the project?
- What are the test and acceptance criteria for the deliverables?
- What is the procedure for receiving the deliverables' final inspection release certificates?
- Are there any technical passport requirements for the deliverables?
- What are the document submittal procedures to the customer?
- Are the documents in dual language?
- What are required file formats and file format revision levels for engineering document submittals?
- Who are on your customer's project team? Do you know their functions and reporting structure?
- Do you know your company's competitors for this project? What are their strengths and weaknesses?
- Are all the application tools at the foreign project site compatible with yours?
- Are all the communication tools at the foreign project site compatible with yours?

Chapter 2

Who Is an International Engineering Project Manager?

If you are leading a project team to design magnetic heads for a disk drive in the United States—getting them fabricated in Malaysia and assembled in South Korea, shipping them to your customer in Japan, and camping in your customer's facilities in Japan to improve their final product yields—then, as the international engineering project manager, you are definitely being challenged in this quadrangle of a maze.

If you are leading a project team to design, build, and test an equipment system in the United States for a British customer, using critical French suppliers and then shipping the system to Russia for commissioning, then you are an international engineering project manager who is being challenged on top of everything else by the dual language and the Russian technical passport requirements.

Suppose you are leading a project team to design, build, test, and deliver 40-feet electric buses for public transportation for a metropolitan transportation district in the United States, and you have two customers, namely, the metropolitan transportation district and the U.S. Department of Transportation. The bus frames are subcontracted to be designed and built in Germany. Then you have quite a few challenges in integration of components due to mixture of metric and English units and transportation of large frames without being damaged from Germany to the United States for final assembly and test.

Cultural and language differences between the customer, the subcontractors, the final product user, and your project team multiply the gravity of the tasks exponentially. A good international engineering project manager should know the historical rivalries and animosities between the countries he is dealing with. He should be cognizant of the political climate in all the countries that are part of the project. You should also inform your team members about pertinent political factors. The United States might be ready to place an embargo on a country that is a crucial part of the project. If your Japanese customer is going to your supplier in Korea for final acceptance of a subassembly for the project, you better join them so that historical rivalries between the two countries do not hamper your project.

Principal Responsibilities

In this quadrangular international maze, the international engineering project manager is responsible for quality and timeliness of deliverables, specifications performance, schedule performance, cost performance, margins, revenue generation (cash flow), team training, team issues and team performance, subcontractors' issues and their performances, risk assessment, intellectual property assessment, project team/customer/subcontractor communications, scope changes, and customer satisfaction and progress reporting. Details of these principal responsibilities are given later in the execution phase of the book. At the beginning of a project you should clearly identify your project responsibilities with your manager.

For example, as an international project manager, you might not be responsible for your project subcontractors' issues and performance. However, you have to work with your company's purchasing group to get all the subcontractors' issues resolved for your project.

In another example, you might not be responsible for test and inspection of the equipment your team is designing and building. You have to work with your quality group for test and inspection functions.

Even with these interdepartmental matrices, you will have the ultimate responsibility for the overall project. For example, during a computer component factory setup project in Singapore, a U.S. company sent a senior project manager to Singapore as an advisor along with his family. This senior project manager advised the Singaporean project manager and his team for a year. The senior project manager's main function was to train the Singaporeans in the U.S. company's project management techniques, especially in time management and risk management. This senior project manager also reported to the general manager of the Singapore facility during the period of this assignment.

Link between Technology and Business

The international engineering project manager is also a link between science, technology, and business. If a project is highly scientific or of leading-edge technology, it is advisable to have twin project leaders—one technical project manager and one business project manager. Successful projects of twin leadership were witnessed in safety vehicle design research, magnetic recording head design, and data communication module design. The chemistry between the two project leaders has to be perfect. They have to live like Siamese twins and support each other without any reservation. This dual project leader concept also brings stability and continuity to the project during vacations, during absences of one of the project leaders from the office, and during reassignments in the middle of the project.

Sometimes you might go into a meeting at the customer's site to discuss technical issues only. However, you will be confronted with nontechnical questions regarding product cost, contract agreement, legal issues, etc. For example, when an international project manager went to his Japanese customers to discuss technical improvements regarding magnetic recording heads, magnetic head prices, production capacities, the topic of the portion of production capacity that can be available to them always came up. The best approach is to take notes and pass the questions to your sales coordinators. However, always follow up with the sales coordinator to make sure that a response has been sent to the customer before the promised action item completion date.

In another case, when visiting a subcontractor in France for a design review meeting, material cost increase and delay in delivery issues came up. This was a very critical item that would have delayed the whole project. The international project manager waited until it was afternoon in France and called his purchasing agent in the U.S. office, who was in charge of the subcontractor, first thing in the morning as the latter came into his office. The project manager discussed the critical situation with the purchase manager and made him hop on a plane and come to France to resolve this critical issue.

Resource Utilization

An international project engineer should be able to utilize all the people in the company (outside his team) in order to solve a critical issue. First, you should go to the person to ask for his help. If he is busy and puts your request under the pile of things he has on his plate, go to his supervisor to get priority. If this does not work, you can go all the way up to the top person to prioritize your issue. Never give up because your project is in jeopardy.

In an example case, the quality engineer who was assigned to the project was overworked due to shortage in the quality department. He could not prepare the product inspection documents in time. These documents had to be approved by the customer in Finland before production could start. Working with the quality department manager did not show any progress to the project manager's satisfaction. He went to the president of the company with a proposal, namely, to put a team of two production inspectors to write the product inspection documents. After the documents were written, these two inspectors were to sit down with the quality engineer and review them before releasing them into document control. The president saw the urgency of the situation, called the supervisor of the two inspectors, and asked him if his two inspectors could be assigned to his project for two weeks to complete the documents. The two production inspectors wrote the documents, and the quality engineer reviewed them together in a working meeting. Finally, the documents made it to the customer in Finland in the nick of time for their approval so that the production could start as scheduled.

You should be cognizant of all the domestic and international resources in your company that can help you technically during your project. This list should also include outside technical consultants.

In some cases, your customer's company or your subcontractor might have a technical resource that will be a lifesaver when you are stuck in one of your tasks. For example, for the design of control consoles that will be operated in hazardous areas, the electrical engineer in charge was a novice right out of school. On the other hand, the subcontractor who built the consoles had an engineer very experienced in designing electrical circuits in hazardous areas. The project manager used the subcontractor's engineer as a consultant and as a checker for all the control console designs. This combination helped groom the young engineer fast and also helped eliminate costly errors in the designs.

Team Leader

The international engineering project manager has to be a good project team leader. A good leader is also a good listener. He or she has to listen to team members and company officials, to customers' comments, subcontractors, and consultants and then make a decision. For example, an international project team designed a 2-rotor, 70 HP at 5000 r.p.m., rotary internal combustion engine for a passenger car from the ground up in 18 months. Prototypes were built in England. During the manufacturing of the prototypes, one of the machinists who was drilling the oil pressure-regulating valve hole for the oil pump observed that the designed hole size was too small in diameter as compared to the other ones that he had seen. Immediately, the project manager called his designer and asked him to review his flow loss calculations and verify the pressure-regulating valve hole diameter. The machinist was correct. The designer had to increase the diameter of the pressure-regulating valve hole and update all the related drawings.

For another project, the project manager was in a project review meeting with a customer in the United States regarding magnetic recording heads. The customer's physicist gave the project manager a couple of tips as to how to reduce magnetic flux leakage losses in magnetic recording heads. The project manager listened to him and changed the head design. This change produced a much more efficient magnetic recording head and provided the customer a leading-edge product.

On another occasion, a milling operator was having difficulty in verifying the finished dimensions of a part according to the drawing and was complaining about it. It was taking him a long time to verify the finished dimensions with the tools he had. He had to build 64 parts for the project. The project manager called in the designer to work together with the milling operator and to re-dimension the drawing so that the finished dimensions could be verified more easily. The designer updated the drawing according to the milling operator's recommendations and released it. Listening to the milling operator saved valuable time and cost for the project.

A good team leader is a high motivator, an efficient information filter, a protector, an ambassador, a timely problem solver, a determined project driver, and an accurate time manager.

Team Motivator

Motivating the team should be a project manager's highest priority. The project manager has to make sure that his team is working in unison and there are no rivalries or animosities among team members. The project manager should give the correct dose of attention to every team member. A junior team member or a remote team member might need detailed guidance as compared to a senior engineer who needs little interference. Sometimes the tables might be turned, and the senior team member might need a lot of attention.

The project manager has to make the international team members feel part of the team. He has to treat them the same way he would treat his home team members, while respecting their traditional and economical factors. For example, the project manager had a young female engineer working on his team in Malaysia. She was shy, but she was an excellent engineer for details and for getting a task done on time. She was always wearing a scarf on her head due to her religious beliefs. You were not supposed to shake hands with her. The project manager learned about it and informed all his team members about this sensitive issue and asked them to respect her wish. She became a very productive member of his project team, and she always felt respected in the team environment.

In dealing with many people from different cultures, you learn that, in every culture, family is very important. Your international project team is a family within itself. You get close to your Korean team members by sharing your family pictures with them. You get close to your Japanese team members by inviting them to your house for dinner instead of taking them out to a restaurant.

A project manager has to gain the respect of his or her team members. You should not favor one team member to another. The promises you make to your team members should be kept and should be finalized on time. A project manager should not promise things that are outside his control, i.e., salary increases, bonuses, extra vacation time, etc. You should respect your team members' cultural backgrounds and cultural needs, and yet be firm with them. You should be able to separate friendship from professional relationship. If a team member is struggling with his tasks, help that person or get help for him or her. If a team member does not like what he or she is doing, talk with that person and with his or her supervisor to move that team member to another project so that he or she can be more effective and motivated and so that the project does not suffer from the person's poor performance.

A project manager is the team builder, both domestically and internationally, which is the nucleus for team motivation. You have to work together with your team in a visible fashion, that is, not behind closed doors. You do not leave your team members working long hours and weekends while you go and enjoy your tennis or golf. You bring in working lunches and dinners, and all go out and have a beer together after a tough day's work. You help your team members go through hurdles. You brainstorm and give direction to young engineers. You make sure that the new direction becomes their idea. You try to avoid the not-invented-here (NIH) factor. You do not force something down their throats. You should be firm, but you should not be a dictator. If there is an error made, you do not penalize the culprit, you do not yell, swear, or scream. You should collect the team, have a lessons-learned session, and take action so that the same error does not occur again. You should praise achievements in front of the whole team. You should go out and celebrate after you've achieved tough milestones.

In one of the projects, a British customer's representatives were visiting the U.S. plant for system acceptance tests. During the week, the Liverpool soccer team was playing for the European championship game. The project manager took his British colleagues and his project team to a sports bar for a two-hour lunch and watched the game. Liverpool won the game, and the British chaps were ecstatic. It was also a good occasion for the project team members to interact with the customer's representatives. The system acceptance tests went smoothly. Maybe the project manager was lucky that Liverpool won.

Let us say, for example, that a team member wants to write a paper on a project-related subject that he or she has researched, has made calculations, and has come up with some good results. If there are other people on your team who contributed even an iota to the paper, recognize them and thank them in the paper. If there are significant contributors, then they should be coauthors to the paper.

A similar situation goes for patents. If a team member comes up with an innovative idea, and he or she has brainstormed this idea with other members of your team who provided some constructive inputs, have him or her share the patent, that is, coauthor the patent with all the team members who contributed. Patent recognitions should be a special event in a company where company executives should be present. Patents should be highly encouraged in a company. Especially in a project team environment with synergy, good things are innovated.

An international engineering project manager should encourage his team members to write technical papers and apply for patents.

Choosing Team Members

Mostly, a project manager does not have a say in choosing the project team members. You will have some stars, some mediocre people, and even some deadwood on your project team. As an engineering project manager with no supervisory authority over a bunch of these multidisciplined and international characters, you have to light a fire under them. Get them awarded for good performance. Praise them during the team meetings. A pat on the shoulder and "job well done" praise noticeably increase the performance of a team member. The project manager should give them small tokens for their accomplishments and for special occasions, i.e., successful milestone luncheons or dinners, gift certificates for their favorite pastimes such as golf, sports events, etc.

In an ion mill release-to-production project for wafer fabrication, the equipment engineer on team was working very hard to complete the acceptance tests. Always little things were coming up, and delay after delay was jeopardizing the wafer production ramp. The equipment engineer was an experienced senior engineer. He was very conscious of the dire situation. He put in an 80-hour week and released the equipment to production. The project manager brought him pizza dinners and helped him in ancillary little tasks so that he did not lose his focus during this ordeal. After successful completion of the project, they went out and had a couple of beers, and the project manager presented him with an 18-hole golf certificate to one of the exclusive golf courses because the engineer was an avid golfer. Also, the project manager wrote an excellent review for the engineer and gave it to his supervisor for the exceptional extra effort that he put in.

As a project manager, you do not have any supervisory functions, namely, no reviews, no hiring or firing powers. You have to deal with people who report to other managers. However, you should contribute to performance and salary/bonus reviews through each team member's supervisor. All the supervisors and team members should be aware of this function that you have and accept it. You also have to know the performance and salary/bonus review procedures in different countries that your company has divisions in.

More often than not a supervisor can come and ask his engineer who is on your team to do a small task for him or her without your knowledge. This action might put a dent in the progress of your project. Most engineers tend to go along with their supervisor's request because he or she is the boss. You have to make sure that tasks and priorities regarding your project are not altered by a team member's supervisor. You have to discuss this issue with all the supervisors and team members and be very firm about it that only you should be able to change tasks and priorities and give assignments to your team members. Control of interference in your team's manpower especially gets difficult for remote and international team members. Also, cultures play into this issue. As an example, in Japan and in Korea, you can very seldom challenge a request from your supervisor.

A plant manager in Korea reassigned a member of the project team to another job without discussing it with the project manager. This shift caused a major setback in the manufacturing start-up project. The project manager learned the hard way to discuss with the supervisors of every member of his international team before a project started, not to reassign the project manager's team members, and not to give them extra tasks without discussing it with him first. If you cannot get your point through and reassignments keep happening, go to top management and prevent your project from failing.

You as the project manager have to push and lobby for the project team members that you want and need on the team, both locally and in foreign countries, because you are the owner of the project and have the total project responsibility. Getting these project team members trained for their deficiencies is also your responsibility. For example, if your customer is in Japan, it is advisable to have a couple of Japanese engineers on your project team to close the language gap, the cultural gap, and the response time.

For the projects with Japan for the computer industry, the project manager hired several young Japanese engineers and brought them to the United States for a year for training. They came to the United States with their families and stayed in company apartments. Training in design and test procedures and learning the magnetic recording technology details for a year was invaluable for them. They also improved their command of English. At the end they became very productive team members for the Japanese customers' projects.

The project manager was putting together a new project team in Malaysia in order to set up a manufacturing line for magnetic recording heads. The engineers on the new team had very little knowledge of magnetic recording heads' working principles and their applications, and statistical process controls. These twelve engineers had to be brought up to speed fast. The best way to train them was on location. The project manager drafted a senior quality engineer to go with him to Malaysia and to train the new engineers on statistical process control. The project manager did the honors on magnetic recording principles and applications. Four hours of intensive training a day for two weeks was a eye-opener for the Malaysian engineers. The project manager and the senior quality engineer gave the Malaysian engineers more than enough dosage of training to perform well for the production start-up team.

Information Filter

Most people do not perform well under extreme pressure. You should be a filter for your team members and filter out the pressures that come from the customers or from upper management. You know what your team members can achieve. You should not overload them, burn them out, and make them throw in the towel. You should help them prioritize their tasks; don't make them jump from one task to another and reduce their efficiency. Sometimes you should become a fatherly figure when it comes to family issues that affect their performance. He or she might be getting divorced or getting married. These two extreme excitements in life affect performance. You should work with them to minimize the effects of these family anxieties on the project.

In data communication module design for a German company, a senior design engineer came to work at 8 a.m. and left work at 5 p.m., not at 5:01 p.m. This was his mode of operation. He would not alter it even if the world was coming to an end. There was a design review meeting coming up with the German customers in two days. The project was behind in several design tasks that this engineer was responsible for. The project manager summarized all the tasks that needed to be done during the upcoming design review and had a heart-to-heart discussion with the senior design engineer as to how to close this gap and get ready for the customer. The project manager proposed to him that he should stay at work until midnight the next two days and complete his tasks in exchange for a full day of vacation after the design review meeting. The project manager made sure that the engineer's supervisor agreed to his proposal beforehand. After some discussions and soul searching, the senior design engineer agreed to the project manager's proposal and stayed longer hours to complete his tasks before the Germans arrived.

One of the engineers on a subsystem design team for an offshore oil platform project could not focus on the job to complete a software program that was crucial for the integration and testing of the components. He was a versatile engineer and was being called on left and right for help. His task was becoming critical to the project. The project manager had to filter out all the noise around him. After discussing with him how to remedy the situation, the project manager unhooked the phone in the engineer's office and put up "DO NOT DISTURB" signs in front of his cubicle so that he could complete the software. This worked for a while but people started to sneak in and ask him for his advice and defocus him again. Then, after discussing with the engineer, the project manager sent him home to work from there for a week to complete his task, and this proved effective.

Some of the software design engineers on a data communication module design team avoided the day shift, and they came to work after the day shift went home in order not to be disturbed and to focus on their tasks. Such an arrangement puts more strain on the project manager because of his having to deal with team members in two shifts, but it is worthy. In addition of completing their tasks on time, these night owls were able to, in real time, communicate with the customer in Germany and get clarifications to ambiguous specifications.

A project manager is like a network server with an effective filtering function. Information comes in from many directions, i.e., customers, subcontractors, regulatory agency design certifiers, regulatory agency inspectors, domestic and international team members, company departments, etc. He or she filters this information and directs it to the people who need it. Filtering of information is very important because you do not want to inundate everyone with irrelevant information and waste valuable project time.

For example, in offshore oil platform subsystem design, build, test, and install projects, there were volumes of technical specifications and applicable international standards. The project manager summarized some of these documents for relevant information and also got some of them summarized by the experts in their particular fields. He organized these technical specifications and applicable standards for every designer on the team. If a designer did not need the paint specification, the project manager did not bother him with the summary of these specifications. If a designer did not need the seismic requirements, he did not waste his time reading the seismic requirements summary. This type of approach helped the design engineers to focus on their portion of the specifications and standards and thus save valuable time for the project.

A project manager also has to be business savvy. Your management should have great confidence in you. Your customer, your subcontractors, and your team should have great confidence in you. You should not squeeze your subcontractors so that your company will make a little more profit. Your purchasing agent has conflicting interests with your project management objectives. He wants to sign up the lowest cost subcontractor, but you want the subcontractor who will deliver on time and within the technical specifications even if the cost is a little higher. You as the project manager should have a say in choosing important subcontractors.

You should not hide issues from your customer. Also, you do not have to disclose every small thing to your customer and get them excited on issues that might be solved internally in a couple of days. You have to know when to filter information and how much to filter to your customer.

In an equipment design, build, test, and delivery project for a computer manufacturer in Japan, the project manager informed the customer of all the potential delays and significant issues in a timely manner. They appreciated his candid and timely inputs. These interactions gave a lot of confidence to the customer. They knew exactly when an equipment was going to arrive in Japan or how much it would be delayed. This close interaction made the customer readjust their production start-up planning and schedule very effectively. At the end of the project, they sent the project manager a very nice thank you note along with a stainless steel vacuum beverage bottle as a token of their thanks.

Let us imagine, for instance, that there is a tool crash at your subcontractor's machine. A part is damaged and is not usable. The subcontractor has to get new material and start all over to machine this part. This might delay delivery of a critical component. Do not rush to the customer. First find out all the details. Discuss all the options to rebuild the part. If need be, help the subcontractor to find the material, and help him financially to get to his feet. Create a new schedule with the subcontractor. Take precautions so that this mishap does not occur again. For example, ask him to use an experienced machinist on your job and change the cutter more frequently. After all the facts are in place, go to your customer and relay the issues and the resulting delay. Do not appear in front of your customer with any unknowns, such as the new ship date, and without a solid and acceptable solution.

Also, if the impact is significant, do the presentation in person, not by e-mail or by telephone. Half the battle in project management is to gain the trust of all the people that are affected by your project. When a word comes out of your mouth, everyone who is involved with the project should believe you and trust you.

Team Protector

As an international engineering project manager, you should be cognizant of all the liability and medical insurances that cover your personnel and your customers when they travel offshore. For example, a customer was dehydrated from diarrhea in South Korea and was admitted to a hospital. He had to be airlifted to the United States after a week of initial recovery in a South Korean hospital. His medical expenses were covered by his company's insurance. In another example, one of the project engineers got into a serious car accident in Malaysia. He was in a Malaysian hospital for two weeks. The liability suit involving the accident was settled in Malaysian courts and all expenses were covered by his company's liability insurance. It is advisable not to drive in a foreign country when you are on a project mission. You, your team members, and customers should get around in driven company vehicles or in public transportation.

As an international engineering project manager, you should be cognizant of all the visa requirements, passport duration validity requirements, and international vaccination requirements. For example, if you are sending an engineer who has a foreign passport to another country, that country's visa requirements are more than likely to be different from that for an engineer who has a U.S. passport. In an interesting case, a foreign engineer was sent to Japan from the United States with the appropriate visa. The project manager asked him to travel urgently from Japan to South Korea to look into a time-sensitive task. The engineer flew to South Korea but could not get into the country because of the special visa requirements. The engineer had to fly back to Tokyo and had to appear at the South Korean consulate in Tokyo to get his visa, and fly back to South Korea again. He lost three days of precious project time during this ordeal.

In one of the projects, a design engineer had to spend two months in South Korea for training and installation of an equipment into a system. The two-month period was unfortunately in November and December. Installation extended his stay into January. He was starting to get burned out. After daily therapeutic phone calls, he agreed to stay on to complete his assignments. He missed Thanksgiving, Christmas, and New Year's Day holidays with his family but completed his assignments successfully. The project manager discussed these holiday sacrifices he made with the design engineer's supervisor and made the supervisor agree to a week of company-paid family vacation in Hawaii for him. This was quite a morale booster for this dedicated engineer.

Scope Changes

As the project manager, you have to control all the changes and deviations from specifications. You have to be the final authority that approves any engineering change order that is related to the project. This change might be in a manufacturing process in Malaysia, or a specification deviation for a French subcontractor, or a replacement component change in Russia. You have to be on top of all the changes for the project. You should coordinate closely with your sales, purchasing, quality, or any other related departments regarding the change but have the final signature on the change release process from document control.

There are cases where salespeople make promises on the fly to the customer and cause a lot of grief in the execution of the project. In such a case, in order to be able to win the bid, a sales manager for a system project for an offshore oil platform promised trolley rails as deliverables for the project without ironing out all technical specifications, design and material costs, and durations as inputs. This was a very demanding project with very low operational temperature requirements in a highly seismic location. Designing the rails under these extreme environmental conditions, finding the right materials, and manufacturing them to tight flatness callouts caused uncalled-for stress on the project team and on the subcontractor.

A project manager should have the final word in negotiating a change from the technical point of view with customers or subcontractors. For example, a customer wants the electronic enclosures to be all stainless steel, and your standard control consoles are stainless steel with plastic windows. If you can convince the customer to use plastic windows, it will be cheaper for your company and you do not have to change the control console enclosure design. You start negotiating with the customer to get an approval for the plastic windows, and the customer says that an ultraviolet (UV)-resistant plastic window will be acceptable. You have to search for all the available UV-resistant plastic window material. Luckily, you find the UV-resistant General Electric (GE) Lexan material that can easily replace the existing windows without any cost penalties. You have to gather all the material data sheets and UV-resistance characteristics from GE and send it to the customer. Then you call the customer and discuss all the relevant aspects of this new window material. The customer is very pleased with the extensive search and meeting their requirements. They finally accept the GE Lexan window for the electronic enclosures. This type of complete interaction with the customer encourages the customer to accept the proposed design change, saves your company time and money, and also keeps the customer satisfied.

In negotiations, you have to be fair and try to create a win–win situation. For example, you sent the interface drawings to the customer with information on where the supply and return points will be for the hydraulic equipment. The customer accepted the interface drawings and ordered high-pressure piping to match the supply and return points shown on your drawings. Towards the middle of the project, a team member discovered that the supply and return points had to be moved and relocated due to accessibility and maintainability requirements that were overlooked in the original design. The customer had to change the piping that was already built and delivered. Also during this period, the customer asked the project manager to prepare the cabling holes for the electrical enclosures that were not a part of the contract. You negotiated and bartered the new high-pressure piping costs to the customer with the preparation of the cabling holes for all the electronic enclosures. There were no extensive contract changes, and no high-level signatures were required. You updated three drawings and provided the customer with what they want, and they accepted the new supply and return piping locations.

Team Ambassador

As the project manager, you have to be an ambassador between your customer, your subcontractors, and regulatory agencies. Whenever a customer visits a subcontractor, you or your representative should join them. Whenever a regulatory agency visits your subcontractor or your plant, you have to bring your customer and your representative to the event. You have to manage, and be prepared for, all these interrelationships.

For example, you might have to prepare your subcontractor in Japan for a U.S. customer visit for a product qualification. If you feel that your subcontractor is not up to it, you have to go to Japan a couple of days early and go over every item related to your project such as the quality plan, ISO requirements, test requirements, traceability requirements, etc., and audit your subcontractor like your customer will and prepare the subcontractor for the upcoming big event. Some international subcontractors might not have been through the wringer of a qualification audit by a U.S. company.

Communication

As the international engineering project manager, you have to direct and store all the communication related to the project. You have to prepare all the schedule and cost performance indices for the project and present them to your upper management. You have to be the ultimate detailer who makes sure that nothing falls through the cracks all the way around the world. Filing all communication with customers, with major subcontractors, with regulatory agencies, with teams in other foreign sites, and with consultants in a chronological order is a must. You should also have backups for these files. For a two-year project with a customer in the United Kingdom, the customer's project manager changed twice. The project manager had to bring the newly assigned customer's project managers to the United States and train them on the history of the project. When the project manager showed the new managers his well-organized project files, they were very impressed. For the documentation they needed for any decision made regarding the project, they relied on his files. Even the customer's document controllers relied on the project manager's drawing release dates, revision dates, and customer approval dates.

Another type of communication is between the project team members. The project manager acts as a communication server among the domestic and international team members. A good example of this was in a three-month wafer fabrication project. The team was developing a new wafer etching process working three eight-hour shifts. Two engineers worked the day shift (7 a.m. to 3 p.m.), two engineers worked the evening shift (3 p.m. to 11 p.m.), and another two worked the graveyard shift (11 p.m. to 7 a.m.). It was crucial that information be exchanged face to face regarding what transpired during every shift for the new process. The project manager had three meetings a day for handover of information from one shift to the next. One meeting was from 6:30 a.m. to 7:30 a.m., the next one was from 2:30 p.m. to 3:30 p.m., and the last one was from 10:30 p.m. to 11:30 p.m. The project manager attended all the meetings. He took the meeting notes and released them as controlled documents. These face-to-face meetings gave the team continuity and synergy in the project and saved it from repeating errors.

Problem Solver

As the project manager, you are the ultimate problem solver. For example, the design specifications for the bronze overlay of trolley wheels (nonsparking wheels due to friction in hazardous zones) were tough to manufacture. You could not find a supplier who could do the bronze overlay according to your tough specifications. You had high hardness requirements, too much bronze thickness, and a difficult overlay profile. You called in several bronzing experts and discussed the manufacturing issues and the tough specifications with them. In parallel, your team had searched and found the best bronze overlay manufacturer in the country. You discussed the design and manufacturing issues with your subcontractor and respecified the bronzing material, and lowered the hardness and the thickness requirements by about ten percent. Also, your team redesigned the bronze overlay profile according to your subcontractor's recommendations. You updated all the affected drawings with an engineering change order (ECN). The subcontractor delivered all 24 bronze overlaid wheels on time and within specification.

In a data communication module design project, it was very difficult to clarify all the specifications and get customer's approval on clarifications in a timely manner as the design phase of the project progressed. The project manager set up daily teleconferences at 8 a.m. from his office to the customer's project manager, 5 p.m. local time in Germany. Also, several team members opted to work at night, and they were in communication with the customer in real time. All specification clarifications were documented and e-mailed to the customer's project manager for his approval. After the customer's approval, these clarifications were entered into the company's and customer's document control systems as addendums to the original project specifications.

Another example is from the new six-inch wafer fabrication start-up project. Your plate and etch group senior engineer was going through a divorce and child custody settlements. He was an experienced engineer with good judgment and systematic solutions to technical issues. You listened to all his personal problems and allocated time after hours for him. Together, you came up with a good solution. You were able to get him to stay at a company apartment for several months while his issues were resolved. You were able to negotiate an appropriate work schedule for him with his supervisor. All this was to keep the project moving smoothly and help this excellent engineer get through difficult times.

Project Driver

A project manager has to be the ultimate driver of the project. For example, a simple and daily schedule-reminding discussion with a designer is always good and brings out issues that have to be solved immediately without wasting time. For example, the task of finite element analysis calculations had to be finished in a week. You asked the designer during your daily and one-on-one mini status meetings, "How is it going? You think we will make it by next week?" His response was "My runs are taking too long. I wish I had another workstation and a software key so that I can run two load cases in parallel. Then I can finish my task according to schedule in a week." You told him that you will get him what he needed that day. You went to the IT (information technology) people, pleaded with them, and tracked them every step of the way in order to get this designer what he needed the same day as promised. He eventually finished his task in a week even if he had to work extra hours.

In another project, one of the subcontractors was having difficulty with a third-party material certification laboratory. The subcontractor was getting low priority in his material certifications and could not start the job without these certificates. Delay for the job was looming in the horizon. The project manager got his purchasing manager to get involved with the case and help remedy the situation. By offering overtime and sharing the overtime costs, material coupons were tested and certificates were issued on time.

For yet another project, a subcontractor who was three time zones ahead was building six heavy equipment transportation vehicles according to the project team's design. The subcontractor was having issues in understanding some of the dimensioning and views in design drawings, and he also found some errors in them. The project manager set up a daily teleconferencing with the subcontractor that included the purchasing agent, the team's two design engineers, and himself. The subcontractor's questions were answered in a timely manner, and the errors he found were corrected immediately. Revised design drawings were released through document control in a day and e-mailed to him. The subcontractor felt like a part of the project team. He knew that the project manager would do anything in his power to keep him sailing smoothly. He delivered the vehicles on time and according to specifications.

On another occasion, a regulatory agency required the materials and their certificates that were used in a project in a specially formatted spreadsheet and in British units. The subcontractor in Italy had difficulty understanding how to convert the material properties into British units, inputting them into the specially formatted spreadsheet, and submitting them to the project manager for completion and submission of the overall design package to the regulatory agency. The project manager asked the subcontractor to submit the raw material data in metric units. He then asked a team member to convert the units and filled the regulatory agency forms appropriately for the subcontractor. This might seem like a small and obvious gesture, but it was a major issue for the subcontractor.

Project Honeymoon Period

An international engineering project manager should not waste the project honeymoon period as would a novice project manager. Get an extension from your customer if the scope changes. Change team personnel if a team member's performance is lagging. Control your subcontractor and be on top of his performance diligently. Always keep the pressure on, but do not overdo it and burn your people out. The stress levels during an international engineering project phases can be characterized as shown in Figure 2.1, depending upon the experience of the program manager. A novice project manager spends an enormous amount of time

STRESS LEVELS	PROPOSE PROJECT	PLAN PROJECT	START PROJECT	MIDDLE PHASE OF PROJECT	FINAL PHASE OF PROJECT	COMPLETE PROJECT	CLOSE PROJECT
VERY HIGH							
HIGH		XXXXX		XXXXX	XXXXX	XXXXX	
NORMAL	XXXXX		XXXXX				XXXXX
LOW							

Novice Project Manager

Experienced Project Manager
XXXXX

Figure 2.1 Stress levels versus project phases with different experience levels of project management.

in preparing a technical proposal for a project because he or she is new to the technology or cannot use segments from old technical proposals. Such a project manager has to create everything from scratch. More time and effort is spent on preparing a technical proposal before a deadline, and stress levels can go up fast. Many technical proposal teams work into early hours of a day to complete it and be able to FedEx it or hand carry it to the customer. Also, a novice project manager listens to all the inputs, and the technical proposal sees a lot of revisions until the last minute before it comes into its final form for delivery.

During the project planning phase, a novice project manager relaxes a little in order to cope with planning the project. He or she might have difficulty in arm wrestling some of managers to get chosen people on the project team. Some of the players might be wrapping up another project and might not be available for his project for a while. Some of the players might need extensive training for the new project. The novice project manager might not know all the significant players in the international sites. All project team personnel issues will add delays to the start-up of a project. The project manager will not know all the subcontractors, and their issues and delivery dates. All these unknowns delay project scheduling. You have to create an initial project schedule with the best inputs you have.

Also, creating a summary of the project specifications might take a longer time for a novice project manager, especially if he or she is new to the technology. Understanding specifications and clarifying the gray areas will take a while. He or she might miss some of the crucial specifications and gloss over them, or brand them as items easy to take care of that might come to bite him or her during the execution phase of the project.

Creating the work breakdown structure, the information management system, creating the cost and schedule performance indices, and having project kickoff meetings with the team members both locally and internationally can be highly stressful for a novice project manager. On the other hand, team members will have low stress levels because of the lack of sufficient project supervision or because of the start-up unknowns in the project.

The best approach to planning of a project for a novice project manager is to get help from the experienced personnel in the company. Get help for summarizing technical specification from seasoned engineers. Get help for work breakdown structure from your finance department. Get help to set up international site teams from the international site general managers. Get help for setting up your information management system from your IT department.

While a novice project engineer is struggling to start the project, everyone on the team starts to acclimate to the new project and try to finish leftover tasks from previous projects. So, inefficiencies creep in fast, and the project enters a honeymoon period where everyone feels that he or she has a great deal of time and can start a task tomorrow or the next day. This start-up period of a project is a critical one where precious time is wasted. Tasks start to pile up and delays start to appear in the horizon. Because schedule performance and cost performance of a project are directly related, a novice project manager should bring pressure on his or her team members from the start to keep the project on track. If the novice project manager is not firm and buys into these mini-delays in the subtasks all through the middle of the project execution phase, he or she cannot avoid his team members going into a high-stress-level environment as the project milestones start approaching.

A novice international engineering project manager can make mistakes in choosing the right team members and can misjudge their productivities. There can be a latitude and work attitude issue with the productivity of the people in the country you are dealing with. A novice project manager sometimes applies too much pressure and burns out his or her people, or too little pressure so that the tasks drag on. You have to apply the pressure dosage according to every team member's heartbeat.

On top of all this, novice project managers try to do much of the tasks themselves, get overloaded, and burn themselves out. A good example of a novice project manager's burnout occurred before a customers' first article acceptance testing of an electric bus design and manufacturing project. It was to start on a Monday. Customers were coming to the site. All project team members were running hundred miles an hour to complete the final tasks before the testing. Everyone was tired, including the project manager, from working very long hours during the previous couple of weeks. The electric bus was hooked up to the charger, and the batteries were fully charged. The project manager took it upon himself to unhook the charger and drive the bus to the first article test location in the plant. However, he forgot to check all around the bus to make sure that everything was clear. There was a steel pole behind the bus, and unfortunately, he ran the bus into it while backing out. One of the windows broke, and there was also some paint damage. Four assemblers and painters on the team had to work all Saturday and Sunday to repair the bus and get it ready for Monday. The bus was ready for customers on Monday, but the paint was still wet. This extraordinary and unnecessary effort was caused by a burned-out and very tired project manager. He could have asked the customers to delay the testing for a couple of days and given himself and his team a breather. Taking action more cautiously would have avoided any mishaps.

Time and Delay Management

As the international engineering project manager, you have to be a precise, and an accurate and an efficient time manager. For example, if your company is in California, you will start your typical day with teleconferencing or videoconferencing with your customer and your suppliers in Europe. You will afterwards distribute to your team members tasks and issues to be resolved, and request answers from them by midafternoon. Then you will have your daily meetings with your team members. After lunch, you will do your teleconferencing or videoconferencing with your Malaysian production facility. Before you leave for home, you will provide responses to Europe so that the project players in Europe will have all the answers they requested by the morning of their day. From home, you will respond to your Malaysian engineers' emergency off-specification requests by e-mail connected to your company's server system, or you will have a teleconference with your Indian subcontractor. Timewise, you are constantly connected to your international project partners except when you sleep.

Time management is also crucial in meetings. Excessive and unnecessary meetings will eat up a lot of precious project time. Also, your project schedule management can be thrown into a turmoil by unexpected delays. International bureaucracy can bite into your project schedule. For example, unanticipated delays in Russian technical passport issuance can delay shipments of equipment to Russia. It is very common to sweat customs delays, work permit issuance delays, international bank funding releases, etc., in an international project.

Another set of delays can come from your customer. Delays in document approvals, response to technical clarifications, purchase-order revision approvals, etc., have to be dealt with by determined pursuance and by juggling tasks and priorities.

You have to be ready to reshuffle tasks and priorities and report to your upper management and ultimately to your customer all the unexpected delays.

Checklist for Chapter 2
Principal Responsibilities

- Do you know the scope of your principal responsibilities for the project?
- Have you discussed and clarified your principal responsibilities for the project with your management?
- Do you know all the interdepartmental links regarding your principal responsibilities?

Link between Technology and Business

- Is the project technically beyond your capabilities?
- Do you need a technical project manager or a technical project advisor to support you?
- Do you know how much flexibility you have in dealing with the business aspects of your project?

Resource Utilization

- Do you know all the technical resources domestically and internationally in your company that can help you if you run into an issue in your project?

- Do you know all the technical consultants domestically and internationally that can help you if you run into an issue in your project?
- Do you know all the technical resources domestically and internationally in your customer's company that can help you if you run into an issue in your project?
- Do you know all the technical resources domestically and internationally of your subcontracts companies that can help you if you run into an issue in your project?

Team Leader

- Are you listening to all the inputs from the people who are involved with your project?
- Are you motivating, filtering information, protecting, being an ambassador, problem solving, driving, and time managing your team?

Team Motivator

- Are you making international team members feel a part of the project family?
- Does every team member domestically and internationally respect you?
- Can any team member domestically and internationally easily talk to you and discuss any issues with you?
- How are you dealing with people who disrupt team unity?
- How are you penalizing team members who make project-related errors?
- Are you always visible and always available to all the project team members, to your customers, and to your subcontractors?
- Do you leave your team members by themselves in tough times or during long work hours or weekends?
- Do you encourage authoring technical papers and patents among your team members?

Choosing Team Members

- Are you involved in choosing your project team members both domestically and internationally?
- Are you pushing and lobbying for the members you want on your team both domestically and internationally?
- Do you know the technical deficiencies of each team member that will affect the project?
- Have you set up a training plan for all the team members domestically and internationally so that project execution can happen smoothly?

- Are you contributing to performance and salary/bonus reviews of your team members domestically and internationally?
- Are all the domestic and international supervisors and team members clear about review procedures?
- How are you dealing with the supervisors who interfere with the progress of your project by assigning side tasks to their engineers?

Information Filter

- Are you filtering the specifications and standards that each member of your domestic and international team member needs?
- Are you filtering scope changes for each member of your domestic and international team members?
- Are you summarizing and helping to prioritize tasks for each member of your domestic and international team?
- Are you filtering unnecessary information flow to your upper management?
- Are you filtering unnecessary information flow to your customers?
- Are you filtering unnecessary information flow to your subcontractors?

Team Protector

- Do you know the extent of liability and medical insurances that will cover your team members internationally?
- Do you know the visa, passport duration validity, vaccination, etc., requirements for the countries you are dealing with?
- How are you protecting your domestic and international team members in case of extraordinary task loads and family sacrifices?

Scope Changes

- Are you the final sign-off person for all scope changes that affect your project?
- Are you straight with your salespeople so that they do not promise any scope change to your customer without first discussing it with you?
- Are you straight with your purchasing people so that they do not promise any scope change to your subcontractors without first discussing it with you?
- Do you have any authority to make minor scope changes after agreeing with your customer and with your subcontractors without going through a formal scope-change process?
- Do you have authority to barter minor scope changes after agreeing with your customer and with your subcontractors without going through a formal scope-change process?

Team Ambassador

- Are you planning and attending (you or your representatives) all domestic and international meetings with your customers, subcontractors, and regulatory agencies?
- Are you helping your international sites to get prepared for critical meetings with your customers and regulatory agencies?
- Are you helping your domestic and international subcontractors to get prepared for critical meetings with your customers and regulatory agencies?

Communication

- Who among your domestic and international team members can communicate with your customers?
- Who among your domestic and international team members can communicate with your subcontractors?
- Who among your domestic and international team members can communicate with regulatory agencies?
- Do you have a safe storage system set up for all the communications that can be sorted by date and by communicating parties?
- What is your backup storage system for communication documents?
- How are you conducting communication among the project's domestic and international team members?

Problem Solver

- Are you tackling problems in a timely fashion both domestically and internationally?
- Are you leading problem-solving efforts domestically and internationally?
- Are you tackling risk management efforts domestically and internationally?
- Are you bringing in your upper management into solving major problems?
- Are you getting help from all available resources when you are stuck?

Project Driver

- Are you reminding your domestic and international team members in a timely manner about their task completion dates? Do they need anything to achieve their deadlines? Do they see any hurdles on their way to the finish line?
- Are you reminding people from other departments, who are performing some tasks for your project but who are not officially on your project team,

in a timely manner about their task completion dates? Do they need anything to achieve their deadlines? Do they see any hurdles on their way to the
finish line?

- Are you reminding your subcontractors in a timely manner about their task
completion dates? Do they need anything to achieve their deadlines? Do they
see any hurdles on their way to the finish line?
- Are you reminding your customers in a timely manner about their task completion dates? Do they need anything to achieve their deadlines? Do they see
any hurdles on their way to the finish line?

Project Honeymoon Period

- Are you getting help from the experienced people in your company to start a
project on time and on track?
- Are there too many unknowns at the beginning of your project such as available personnel for your team both domestically and internationally, subcontractors, subcontractor delivery dates, etc.?
- Can you put together a reliable project schedule?
- Are you controlling closely the progress of the tasks of your domestic and
international team members from the start of the project?
- Are you controlling closely the progress of the tasks of your subcontractors
from the start of the project?
- Are you controlling closely the progress of the tasks of your customers from
the start of the project?
- What are you doing with nonperforming team members?

Time and Delay Management

- How are you managing your time during a workday in an international
environment with multiple time zones?
- Do you know how many hours each domestic and international site is behind
or ahead of you?
- Do you know if the international sites switch times for daylight savings and
when they do the switching?
- Have you set up fixed-time videoconferences or teleconferences with your
customers, international team sites, subcontractors, and regulatory agencies?
- Are you having efficient and effective meetings?
- Are there items in the international bureaucracy that can cause unexpected
delays?
- Do you have plans as to how to deal with unexpected delays?

Chapter 3

Getting an International Project

Every international project bidding process is different. For company external international projects, you might have to pass successfully the technical bid phase first and then you are allowed to bid the business phase. During the business phase of the bidding, your company might have to excel in several financial metrics, such as cash flow, debt-to-sales ratio, historical performance, etc., before being let in. During the technical phase of bidding, your company might be audited for manufacturing capacity, engineering strength and depth, environmental and safety, ISO procedures, etc., before the bidding.

As an international engineering project manager, you might get involved heavily with the technical proposal preparation and have a little to say on the business phase of the bid. Sometimes the whole bid package is prepared by your sales people. If it is a winning proposal, you might get the project ownership from the start. Sometimes you might be given a project in the middle if the present project manager runs into issues and he or she is removed from an ongoing project by upper management. So, there are many ways to take the reigns of an international project.

Getting Ready to Write a Technical Proposal

This chapter will cover international project technical proposal preparation. First, you should study the whole bid package including all the technical specifications and standards. If there are missing specifications or standards that are listed in the bid package, you should obtain them from the customer. If any of the specifications and standards is in another language, you should get them translated into English. You should take notes and question the areas, both technical and business, that are challenging, do not seem right, not doable, increases the cost, or where an alternative approach might be more feasible. More often than not, the customer throws at you many standards and codes that do not apply to the project. You should take exceptions to specifications and standards that are not feasible or not applicable to the project you are bidding for and discuss them with your customer's technical liaison in order to make sure that you are not deviating from what they are expecting from you in the proposal. You should always get written bid clarifications from your customer.

In international bids, dual-language requirements, unit requirements, system and equipment design and test-certification requirements, regulations, rules, and codes that apply, electrical power requirements, subcontractor requirements, scope change order process requirements, etc., can be very daunting. For example, in one of the bid packages for designing a system for an offshore oil platform, the customer only allowed usage of a certain brand of electric motors. In another example, the customer only allowed usage of tube fittings from a German manufacturer and all other components had to be CE (Certified European) approved. In such cases, you might have to deal with a new subcontractor that you have not dealt before, or it might be difficult to source a CE component that is needed in your system.

You should also know your competition for the international bid. What are their technical strengths and weaknesses? What do you have to do to your engineering team to surpass your competition technologically?

After absorbing all the bid-package requirements, you should form a technical proposal team. This team might include international site members (if there is work to be done on a foreign site), consultants (if you need some technological advantage that is not your forte), and some domestic and international subcontracts who design and build a part of your system. Or you might team up with other companies who might bring strong technological synergy to the party.

You should also know by heart some of the essentials of the bid package. These are the bid due date and time, bid address and the person in charge, and bid submission requirements. If there are any changes to bid due date, it should be obtained in a written form from the customer. It is easy to hear about missed opportunities due to a delay in international flights for a hand-carried proposal or a wrong delivery address on a FedEx package.

In an international offshore oil platform system bid, the sales person called the head of technical proposal team to inform that the customer will surely extend the bid due date by a week. When you receive information similar to that you relax a little on your technical proposal preparation. This information came after a telephone discussion between the sales person and customer's purchasing agent. There was nothing documented about it. At the end, the bid due date was not extended, and it was a major scramble to get the technical proposal finished on time.

A technical proposal on hybrid vehicles was being prepared until 3 a.m. the day it was due. It went through many iterations and comprised five volumes (about four hundred pages). Ten copies of the technical proposal were due at 10 a.m. at the customer's site that was four hours away by driving. Two engineers from the company took the technical proposal copies in a van and made it in time for hand delivery. It was lucky that the van did not break down on its way.

In another occasion, an international engineering manager was hand carrying a communication system technical proposal to Pakistan that was due to open in twenty-four hours. Due to unforeseen flight delays in Singapore and inside Pakistan, he was able to arrive two hours late to the bid opening. The customer was informed ahead of bid-opening time about the unusual situation and luckily was good enough to delay the bid-opening time by two hours.

In most cases, technical proposals are created in short durations. In some international proposals, translation of the proposal might be required. You have to allocate time for translation to the final revision of the proposal during a hectic schedule. It will be good to ask the customer if you can submit the technical proposal both in the required language and also in English.

You should also know by heart all the project milestones, scope of supply, product acceptance criteria, product-shipping requirements, documentation requirements, project liquidated damages, product warranty conditions, and intellectual property (IP) conditions.

How are the project-related inventions, patents, and patent disputes to be handled? International patent applications can get very expensive and time consuming. In the event of an IP dispute between the parties, which countries' laws will be used? What is the language of arbitration? For example, during the preparation of a computer component technical proposal, in the event of a new invention during the project, patent-application countries became an issue. The customer wanted joint patent applications for nine countries. This was very costly and time consuming. Finally, after negotiations, it was mutually agreed to apply for joint patents only in Japan and the United States.

Most international projects are fixed-price and fixed-time projects based on well-defined deliverables. It might take a year or two or more to finalize the selling phase of a project. A bidding process might be voided and restarted again due to many reasons beyond your control. Your customer's project priorities, project scopes, market forces, and project budgets might change. There might be numerous technical and business negotiations with the customer before the contract is finalized. During the selling phase, all communications with the customer and all meeting minutes should be kept in a precise fashion and in a chronological order because, by the time a purchase order is issued by the customer, all the original negotiators of the contract on both sides might have gone to other endeavors. In such a case, it took three years for the customer to award an international contract from the initial request for quotation date.

If you have a sloppy sales department and they do not keep all the sales-meeting records and project-specification clarifications properly, the project is in trouble from the start. Then, your job as the engineering project manager gets much tougher. You have to list all the holes that you see during the negotiations. You have to discuss these holes with the responsible sales people and with the customer to fill in the blanks. If needed you have to go to your upper management and explain to them the gray areas of the project that might cause extra time and cost to the project. For example, in the heat of negotiations, a senior sales person threw in a microscope that the customer needed and said that the company would cover it, not understanding the requirements and the specifications of the microscope. It turned out that the microscope was a very high resolution one, and its cost was \$52,000. The project had to eat this extra cost, and it was not even on the list of deliverables. The engineering project manager informed upper management regarding this situation, and the senior sales person had to find another job.

You should know the final engineering hours that the sales people negotiated down from your original estimates to get the cost down and win the contract. It is advisable to document all revisions of engineering-hour estimates. There have been bid negotiations during which the sales people cut into the engineering hours as much as 50 percent in order to be able to win a contract. You should know the final margin of the project. Does this margin have contingency funds built into it? Some sales groups use project margins and others use project margin multipliers as their profit metrics as defined in the following equation:

$$\text{Project margin} = (\text{Project revenue} - \text{Project cost})/\text{Project revenue}$$

$$\text{Project margin multiplier} = \text{Project revenue}/\text{Project cost}$$

Winning Ways to a Technical Proposal

The technical proposals should have a logical outline that covers what the customer is looking for. An executive summary of the proposal up front always give you positive points from your customer's executives because they do not have to read and absorb volumes of your technical proposal. In a technical proposal, always emphasize your company's strong points and also emphasize how you are going to strengthen your weak segments. You might be teaming up with a company who is strong in chip design or you might be bringing in some high-level consultants in metallurgy from a university. You might be teaming up with a company who has strong balance sheets. The bottom line is that you cannot go in front of your customer with a weak link in your proposal. You should also include your team members', consultants', and subcontractors' resumes in your proposal, emphasizing their accomplishments as related to the proposal technical fields. You should emphasize your international team setup and your international team management procedures. If possible, include engineers on your team from the countries you are dealing with.

You should also point out in your technical proposal the language depth of your team members and your technical translator, if needed during your project. There should be a section on previous related projects including the successes and failures in these previous projects, with lessons learned. On-time delivery is one of the key metrics in a technical project appraisal. Therefore, it is advisable to present a clear schedule-performance index for the previous related projects. In a technical proposal, you have to be careful not to lay out all your IP and give away all your aces. You can list all the relevant patents and research you have done in the past and that is on going now without relaying the details and without stepping onto your other customer's toes. You might have two or more competing customers in front of you and have to play around a fine line between two or more competing customers. This kind of IP protection is a must in leading-edge technology projects. You have to give confidence to your customer that you are very sensitive to bidirectional IP inputs and protect these IP inputs from other competitors.

For example, in an advanced computer component proposal, customer's bid package specifications, drawings, and correspondence documents were kept in a locked safe. Only an engineer who was dealing with the proposal was able to check out a bid document. He or she could not make any copies of the bid-related documents and had to return these documents to the safe before leaving the office.

You should emphasize technologically challenging areas in detail and give alternate approaches or design options without deviating from customer's technical objectives. You should also list advantages and disadvantages of each design option. Costing and schedule estimates for each different design option and how it affects the overall project will take considerable time and effort in completing a technical proposal. However, this kind of detailed approach to technically challenging segments of the project will provide plus points to your company during proposal evaluation.

Internal Projects

Similar goal-based technical proposals can also be used for an internal project. These internal projects have a technical proposal, deliverables, a schedule, costs, return on investment, and a defined team. Mostly, an MS Power Point presentation is made to the upper management for the internal project proposal. If the internal project proposal is significant to the company dollarwise or future-technologywise, the proposal presentation can be made to the board of directors of the company. For example, an automated manufacturing process system proposal was made to the board of directors of a computer company to produce precision computer components in

Malaysia. More than the technology aspects, the board was interested in estimates on the return on investment. The green light was given to the project after numerous scenarios were analyzed for return on investment estimates.

Sometimes you might think that there is no competition to internal project proposals. However, a good company management should consider outside bids to the same internal project proposal, i.e., from different divisions of the company or from outside companies that excel in that particular field.

Another situation arises when your internal resources are saturated with work and your engineering group cannot handle another project, say, a new chip design project. These are called "bubble projects" and are mostly given to outside design companies. Another situation arises when all your designers are at senior level and your hourly rates are going off the roof. In this case, again an internal project might have to be contracted outside in order to meet the budget.

Clarifications

There can be conflicting information in the technical specifications that govern a project. One of the specifications might allow you to design to the material yield strength point, whereas another might allow you to design to 90 percent of the material yield strength point. One of the specifications might call for the equipment top color to be yellow and in another part of the bid package, beige. You have to clarify with the customer the hierarchy of technical specifications. In most cases, the customer throws all the technical specifications and standards in front of the supplier even if they do not apply to the project. Clarify ambiguous and nonapplicable specifications and standards at your technical proposal. Take exceptions before the project starts. Make sure that the customer agrees to all the clarifications and exceptions to their technical specifications and standards in a written form. Verbal agreements mean nothing. This extensive specification and standards review at the bidding phase of the project helps you to uncover some hidden and conflicting information that will affect the project cost and schedule. Also, this detailed review will provide you a good foundation to develop your technical specifications and standards summary for the project, sometimes called the design basis, during the planning phase of the project. If you come across any international standard during this review that you are not familiar with, it will give you some time to digest it. If you are not an expert in a field, let an expert in that field summarize the standard for you.

If you get the project awarded, your first task will be to generate the project design basis. You have to let your team members work with this design basis of the project. You cannot make every member on your international team read every technical specification and standard related with the project.

A typical technical specification package for an international offshore oil platform equipment system design, manufacturing, test, and delivery will contain over

20 specifications with total pages exceeding 500 pages. For example, purchase order and scope of supply, technical specification sheets for each equipment, technical specifications for the system, exceptions to codes and specifications, specifications for instrumentation, specifications for document requirements, specifications for spare parts, material storage requirements, preservation and handling specifications, specifications for units of measurement, procedure for material concession requests, coating specifications, quality assurance and quality control requirements, material certification requirements, nameplate requirements, environmental data sheet requirements, weight and center of gravity data sheets, qualified subcontractor list, Russian technical passport requirements, etc.

Some of these specifications require you to submit the data in the customer's specific format using customer's specific software. For example, instrument data sheets, weight and center of gravity data sheets, spare parts list, etc., can have specific formatting requirements. A customer's specific software needs training, has a learning curve, has bugs, and might cause a lot of headaches during the course of the project. If possible, present your work to the customer in a familiar format to your team. Use a software that your team is primed for. You can, for example, present your data to the customer in an MS Excel spreadsheet, which can then be inserted in your customer's software by the customer. You have to agree on these software, file formatting, and file-transfer procedure issues at the bidding phase or latest at the customer kickoff meeting for the project.

Documentation Requirements

In some projects, the documentation requirements can be overwhelming. You have to agree with the customer on every document that has to be delivered, the delivery dates, delivery formats, softwares to be used and their revision levels, delivery language, etc., at the bidding phase or latest at the customer kickoff meeting for the project.

Weekly progress reports to the customer can be a huge burden. Try to agree on monthly or bimonthly progress reports. If anything significant happens during the month, you have to have a teleconference or a videoconference anyway. Use the customer's format for the customer progress reports.

In addition to the customer progress reports, here are some of the documentation requirements in an equipment system design, manufacturing, test, and delivery project: Master document schedule; project schedule; subcontractors schedules; assembly drawings; interface drawings; electrical and hydraulic schematics; weight and center of gravity data sheets; noise level data sheets; equipment specification data sheets; electric motors performance curves; computer system manuals; computer programs and their logic diagrams; welding procedure specifications; welding procedure qualification records; installation, operation, and maintenance manuals; technical passports, etc.

There is a good ballpark estimate in international system design projects, regarding the documentation, namely 50 percent of the cost of a project goes to the hardware and the other 50 percent to the paperware.

Document review duration by the customer is also a significant parameter in the project contract agreement. Some contract agreements specify up to four weeks for review and response from the customer for the submitted documents. This is a long time schedule because your billing milestones mostly rely on the final approval of the submitted documents. It is advisable not to exceed the document review turn-around time by more than two weeks. Document acceptance levels by the customer are also crucial. In some international projects, milestone payments are released only after a document's full acceptance level is reached, namely "approved without comments" level. Some customers require continuous follow up and pushing for document-review response without annoying them. If the customer's reviewer is a contractor, then you are in deep trouble because customer's contractor's document reviews take longer than normal due to his or her financial gains.

Design Review, Certification, Inspection, and Hold Points

As an international engineering project manager, you have to pay particular attention to design review, inspection, and test hold points of the project. Most design reviews and hold points require a two-week notice to the customer and to the regulatory agency inspectors. You have to be diligent on these notices. Your customer or the inspector will be traveling thousands of miles and come to your facility tired with a jet lag to find out that you are not ready for them. This kind of a situation creates nonconfidence and gives you a black eye that is hard to heal.

Another area of concern is design certification by required regulatory agencies. Do you design the system for the project, submit the documents to the regulatory agency and wait for their approval without starting production? Or do you take the risk and start production of equipment as soon as the design drawings are approved internally and by the customer? Regulatory agency design-approval risk can be minimized by discussing the design with the assigned examiners during the design phase of the project. As long as their codes, concerns, and inputs are treated in the system design, regulatory agency examiners should approve the design without any glitches.

It is much more cost effective to notify a customer's inspector two weeks before the event even if you are not 100 percent sure that the inspection event will occur on a particular date. You can tell him the situation and inform him that you are, say, 90 percent sure that the inspection event will occur. The inspector will make his travel arrangements and reserve his time for you. If the event date moves forward, immediately inform the inspector and reschedule him. If he has any expenses incurred due to this schedule change, pay those expenses. If he comes over to your facility and you are not ready, say, for another day, treat him to a round of golf or a wine-tasting tour. Bottom line is do not call the customer or the inspector at the last minute and show them equipment that is not completely pretested and verified.

Postproject Requirements

As an international engineering project manager, you have to be cognizant of all the postproject requirements in the contract. Installation, operation, and maintenance requirements with agreed upon response times can be an unbearable burden to the company and to your project team. Most installation and training personnel are chosen from the project designers. It is also a good experience for the designers to see their design's successes, failures, and required improvements in the field. Installation, training, and maintenance personnel have to be taught out and included in the project plan. Mostly, the cost of installation and maintenance efforts is separated from the main project cost and agreed with the customer on an hourly basis, including travel expenses.

Same caution goes for the spare parts list. When and who will purchase the spare parts for the project? You need to have a much more comprehensive spare parts list for an international project that is destined for Sri Lanka or Azerbaijan than one in the Gulf of Mexico because of unavailability of simple tools and components, shipping delays, export and import rules, customs delays, etc.

Most projects are evaluated first for the technical content and if you are successful in the technical content, then the business content. A proposal with good technical content and a solid international team and with fair pricing is a sure winner. Customer satisfaction in the previous projects, a good name in your field of expertise, and good financial rating of the company also help to win contracts. Sometimes, as a company, you have to reject an awarded project, if low pricing and tight schedule required by the customer are impossible to achieve. Sales people unfortunately work on bonus systems that force them to bring in projects that are sometimes a bear to finish on time and within budget.

Checklist for Chapter 3

Getting Ready to Write a Technical Proposal

- ■ Have you studied the whole bid package including all the technical specifications and standards?

- Do you have all the missing specifications and standards that are listed in the bid package?
- Do you have all the specifications and standards that are not translated in English?
- Are you taking notes and writing down all the questions and challenges you have in both technical and business sections of the bid package?
- Are you listing all the exceptions and clarifications to specifications and standards you want to discuss with your customer?
- Are you getting written confirmations for all the exceptions and clarifications from your customer?
- Are there single-source subcontractors you have to deal with and are specified in the bid package?
- Do you know who your competition is?
- Do you have weak areas in your technical team that you need to beef up for this proposal?
- Have you formed your technical proposal team?
- Are there contributors from foreign countries to your technical proposal?
- Are there consultants who will contribute to your technical proposal?
- Are there other companies that you have to team up with to enhance your technological edge?
- Do you know all the proposal submission requirements?
- Does the final technical proposal have to be translated into another language?
- Do you know by heart the scope change process requirements?
- Do you know by heart all the project milestones, scope of supply, product acceptance criteria, product-shipping requirements, documentation requirements, project liquidated damages, product warranty conditions, and intellectual property conditions?
- Do you know how the project-related inventions, patents, and patent disputes are to be handled?
- Are you and your sales people documenting all communication and meeting minutes in a chronological order with the customer during the bidding phase of the project?
- Are you documenting all your engineering-hours estimates that you provide to your business people?
- Do you know the profit margin for the bid?
- Is there any contingency fund included in the costs?

Winning Ways to a Technical Proposal

- Are you covering and emphasizing the areas your customer is looking for in your technical proposal?
- Do you have an executive summary in front of your technical proposal?

■ Are you emphasizing your company's and your international project team's strong points?
■ Are you detailing how you are going to strengthen your weak segments?
■ Are you emphasizing your international team setup?
■ Are you emphasizing your international team management procedures?
■ Do you have international members on your team from the countries that you are dealing with?
■ Do you have the language depth on your team or do you need translators for the languages of the countries that you are dealing with?
■ Do you have a section in your technical proposal that covers previous related projects and details the successes and failures with lessons learned?
■ Are you presenting schedule-performance indices from your previous related projects?
■ Are you careful not to give away your intellectual properties in your technical proposal?
■ Are you careful not to give away your other customers' intellectual properties in your technical proposal?

Internal Projects

■ Who are you going to present your technical proposal to?
■ Have you considered several different project approach scenarios?
■ Have you calculated the return on investment for each scenario?
■ Do you have advantages and disadvantages listed for each scenario?
■ Do you have your proposed team members listed by name, by involvement portions of the project, and by involvement durations?
■ Do you have any competition for the proposed internal project?

Clarifications

■ Do you know the hierarchy of technical specifications and standards that are called out in the bid package?
■ Are there any international standards that are called out and that you are not familiar with?
■ Is there any software that is developed by your customer and you have to use during the execution of the project?
■ Do you know all the softwares and their revision levels that will be used during the execution of the project?
■ Do you know how the files will be transferred to your customer and in what format?

■ Have you received all the clarifications in a written form from your customer regarding all the technical specifications, standards, and other issues that came up during the bid-package review process?

Documentation Requirements

■ Do you agree with all the required documentation deliveries during the execution phase of the project?
■ Are you making a counter proposal for the documentation requirements and delivery dates?
■ How often and in what format do you have to submit a progress report to the customer during the execution phase of the project?
■ What is your customer's document review and response time specified in the bid package?
■ At what document acceptance level will your customer release milestone payments?

Design Review, Certification, Inspection, and Hold Points

■ Do you know all the design review, inspection, and hold points for the project?
■ Do you know the locations for the design review meetings? Do you have to travel to customer's international site for the design review meetings?
■ Do you know the design-certification requirements for the project? Who is the design-certifying agency? Have you dealt with them before? Do you know their certification procedures and response times?
■ Do you know the test-certification requirements for the project? Who is the test-certifying agency? Have you dealt with them before? Do you know their certification procedures and response times?
■ How much notice do you have to give to your customer's and to regulatory agency's inspectors for inspections?

Postproject Requirements

■ Are there installation, operation, and maintenance requirements? What kind of personnel you will need to cover these requirements?
■ What is the language for installation, operation, and maintenance manuals?
■ Are there postproject training requirements? Who will do the training at the customer's site? Does the training to be done in the local language?

- What are the spare parts requirements? Are the spare parts only for start-up of the operations or for an extended period such as for four years?
- Do you know the availability of simple tools and components in your customer's international installation site that will be needed during installation, operation, and maintenance of your equipment?
- Do you know the durations and import regulations for shipping simple tools and components to the international installation site?

Chapter 4

Planning an International Project

When the project is given a go ahead by upper management, you have a short time to prepare for its planning. Planning includes selecting team members, forming international teams, creating a summary of the project specifications, creating work breakdown structure, generating a list of tasks, creating the initial schedule, structuring the project information management system, generating a cost and schedule performance spreadsheet, and holding the project kickoff meetings. This initial planning period for an international project manager is a very busy and tough one and might require a lot of international travel in a very short time because the clock for the project starts to tick, and you should take at most a couple of weeks to bring everything together to launch the project domestically and internationally.

Selecting Team Members

The right domestic and international team members are key to the success of a project. You might have to create counterpart teams in a foreign country to execute an international project. Finding the right team leaders and team members in a foreign country can be tricky and very time consuming. As the project manager, interview every team member, domestic and international, face to face, learn their backgrounds, and make agreements with them on their training requirements for the upcoming project. If face-to-face interviews are not possible, perform video-conference or teleconference interviews.

For example, for an automated assembly line equipment that was designed and built in the United States and then installed and operated in Malaysia, the U.S.-based project manager had to form a local team in the Malaysian factory. The project had to also have a strong team in Malaysia who could understand every detail of the automated assembly line equipment and who were confident of tackling any downtime issues, maintenance issues, and training issues for the project to be successful.

The key was to find the right Malaysian team leader with automation engineering background, hands-on capability, and leadership skills. The U.S.-based project manager performed face-to-face interviews in Malaysia with the candidates prescreened by the Malaysian human resources department according to the project manager's criteria. The chosen leader was a Malaysian senior engineer who was assigned to the project full time and reported to the factory general manager with a dotted line reporting to the U.S.-based project manager.

The training of the Malaysian project leader was detailed, scheduled, and executed in the United States. The Malaysian project leader chose his team members, and they were also interviewed by the project manager. The Malaysian team was given the full responsibility to carry out the automation project after a smooth transition from the U.S. team.

Major automation installation and start-up issues were encountered because of insufficient spare parts, inadequate power input controls, and several software glitches. Daily teleconferencing and timely support from the U.S. team, both remote and on location, made the automated assembly line project a success.

Part-time team members are mostly inefficient and always have other conflicting priorities. Some team members might need training in certain skills. Include such training in your project plan. When you have international team members, evaluate their English proficiency and decide if you will need a translator during the course of the project. Include international travel time and time lost due to jet lag in your planning. Some team members might be getting married, availing maternity leave, or having a surgery scheduled. Include all these scheduled special events in your planning. Do not forget to include the team members' vacation plans and planned holidays (domestic and international) in the project plan, and those of your customer's team members. Similar precautions should be taken for the subcontractors. It is hard to find anyone around during August in Europe and in Japan, during Christmas time in the United States, and during Chinese New Year celebrations in the Pacific Basin.

Talk with every team member as if you are interviewing him or her. Maybe some of them will not want to work with you. Understand their strengths and weaknesses. An all-novice team will require a lot of extra effort from the project management point of view to achieve good results. Try to get a well-balanced team with seasoned engineers and with new and dynamic engineers who are willing to learn and contribute. Also, try to include mentoring-oriented duos or trios on your team. For example, an experienced data communication chip software design engineer and a novice one might form a good subteam for your chip software design tasks.

Some of the team members you want might be available for your project at a later date because of their other project commitments or assignments. Shift the task schedules of these team members to see what the late start effects are on the overall project. It is always better to have a team member that you know, want, or have worked effectively together with before.

In a data communication module design project, an average software design engineer was forcibly put onto the team by upper management. The portion of the module that this engineer was responsible for was always being delayed, and there was no light at the end of the tunnel. Even micromanaging him daily did not improve his performance. After several discussions with upper management and three months into the project, he was replaced with a dynamic and highly regarded software design engineer. The project manager had wanted this engineer on his team from the start of the project. The new engineer had to start designing this portion of the module from scratch. A whole three months of effort was wasted, and the cost overrun was never recovered. However, the project was completed two weeks late, and the customer was more than satisfied with the results.

Avoid, if you can, team members who will degrade team harmony and who have had past conflicts with each other.

Agree with the team member's supervisor that you will contribute to his or her performance review. Agree on the extent of your review contributions, i.e., salary increase, bonus, stock option, etc. Make sure the team members are aware of this. Also, an international team member's review criteria would be different from the U.S. team member's. You as a project manager have to know the differences in review metrics.

For some projects you might not have the right personnel in your company, or your company's resources might be saturated; then you have to go outside the company and get consultants or contractors for some of the tasks. Interview the consultants or contractors in detail. Make sure they are capable of performing the tasks you are planning to allocate to them. Always allocate well-defined and easy-to-track tasks. Make sure that their design methods and formats are compatible with your company's, as well as their design tools and revision levels.

In some cases, you might be thrown into the middle of a project where the team is already established and tasks are in progress. In such a case, you have to quickly evaluate all the team members, have one-on-one discussions with every one of them, go over their tasks, and make the necessary adjustments as needed for the success of the project. For example, an international engineering project manager was brought on to straighten out a dynamic design project. After two weeks of reviewing both the domestic and international team members and the status of their tasks, the project manager found amazing deficiencies in the execution of the project. There were overlapping task responsibilities, some engineers did not have sufficient depth of knowledge and training to perform their tasks, document control procedures were weak, and there was animosity between design engineers and the manufacturing department. The project manager took immediate actions to remedy all these deficiencies and brought the project on solid footing in a month.

Creating a Summary of Project Specifications and Standards

The next thing on your list during the planning phase of an international project is to prepare a summary of the customer specifications and standards for the project. This summary should be concise, arranged in a logical fashion, and should follow the customer's scope of supply and hierarchy of specifications and standards. If any of these specifications and standards is in another language, it should be translated first into English.

The project summary (design basis) should be a controlled document. It should start with the project definition, such as the project name, the customer, proposal identifier, work breakdown structure with charge numbers, major subcontractors, consultants, and the project team members with their responsibilities. Delivery dates, late penalties, and early delivery rewards should be outlined at the beginning of the summary.

Then, customer specifications and the applicable standards should be listed in a hierarchical order. These documents should be available to the team members in electronic form if they want to go in and review them in detail. All the specifications should be listed with their revision level and standards with the year of their publication.

When a standard is specified, identify the sections down to the paragraphs that apply to your project. Do not let your team members search through hundreds of pages of standards. It is a waste of time and money for the project.

Specify the applicable units for all the documents. Try to stick to SI units if possible. Dual units are always a source for error. Specify the language requirements. Some documents such as the installation, operation, and maintenance manuals and interface drawings might be in dual language. Try to get these documents generated in English first, and after they are fully approved by the customer, get them translated. The full approval process by the customer might take several iterations.

Step by step summarize the specifications for each item on the scope of supply. Do not forget to include the requirements for the spares. If you are not an expert in a certain field, get help while summarizing the specifications and standards. There might be gray areas and verbal nuances you might misinterpret.

Then, the overall project environmental and utility requirements and the interface requirements should be outlined. A summary of the design review requirements, documents, and calculations should be listed.

Sometimes simple and significant parameters are missed, such as the minimum design temperature. For example, in a structural design project, a –20°C minimum design temperature was mistakenly taken as –20°F, which caused much tougher material property requirements. In another example, some designers overlooked the voltage specifications and called out components such as safety lights, computer printers, etc., to be 120 VAC operation part numbers instead of the correct 240 VAC ones specified by the customer.

These summaries should be followed by the overall project regulatory agency design and test certification requirements, material requirements, fabrication requirements, coating requirements, acceptance test and inspection requirements, delivery requirements, and documentation requirements.

The final section of the project summary should include a list of similar historical projects and lessons learned from these previous projects.

The project specifications and standards summary should not exceed 20 to 30 pages. This document should be reviewed by company managers who are related to the project and released by document control before the project kickoff meetings with team members and subcontractors. It is a good idea to have the customer kickoff meeting before the project summary is finalized in order to iron out all the gray areas with the customer. If this does not happen, you go with the best information that you have and release the project summary document, and if there are changes after the customer kickoff meeting, then you can revise it. This project summary document, is a living document, and it should be revised for all specification changes, scope changes, etc., during the course of the project.

In some projects, generating the specifications with the customer is the initial phase of the project. For example, in an international data communication network layer chip design project, the international standard protocol was the baseline specification. The project team worked together with the customer to define the enhancements to the international standard protocol during the initial phase of the project.

In a research safety vehicle design project, the initial phase of the project was to generate design options and detail their feasibilities for production. After a design option was chosen by the customer, it was detailed in the second phase of the project. The third phase of the project was to build the prototype vehicles, and the fourth phase was to test them around the world. In a way, each phase of the project generated the research safety vehicle for the following phase.

Creating Work Breakdown Structure

The work breakdown structure should be a mirror image of project deliverables. In the work breakdown structure, program management should be a separate cost bucket (subproject number). A deliverable task also should be broken into logical cost buckets such as specification, design, check, design review, manufacturing, and test cost buckets.

A typical work breakdown structure is given for a Malaysian factory setup project in Figure 4.1.

Always agree on the work breakdown structure with the financial department. Any charges to the project cost buckets should be approved by the project manager. These charges can be team member hours, consultant's invoice, purchasing invoice, etc. If you leave the project charge gates open, you will have quite a few erroneous charges to the project. If a company is waiting to get a contract, or if there is a shortage of contracts, you might see some people charging to your project even if you just said "good morning" to them in the hallway.

Make sure that all your domestic and international team members know the project charge numbers they can charge to. They should also know the limits of their charge numbers, namely, how many hours are allocated to that particular charge number. Some engineers think that a charge number is like a bottomless bucket. You have to make sure that you are getting an honest hour's work for an hour allocated to a charge number. Also make sure that the charges are made justly to your project. There can be a lot of mix-ups in charging to a project versus to overhead. The project schedule that will be discussed next should be generated in concert with the work breakdown structure.

Creating the Initial Schedule

There are several ways to create a project schedule. You can put the whole project into one large schedule with hundreds of tasks and dependencies while covering all the resources, namely, domestic, international, subcontractors, etc., and while covering all the milestone dates. This is the way to go if you have a scheduler helping you in the project. Because schedules are dynamic documents, they have to be updated at least weekly. It gets very cumbersome and difficult to find errors in a large schedule. You have to keep each week's schedule as a separate file in order to be able to trace back in case of errors.

If you are a project manager by yourself and trying to generate a project schedule for a large project, i.e., more than, say, 200 tasks, keep the project schedule simple and manageable. First, create a master schedule with milestones, task groups, and dependencies. Every critical date related to a document delivery to the customer, an internal or customer design review meeting, a long lead and hard-to-get component delivery, an acceptance test, shipping, etc., should be on the master schedule. This master schedule is for the upper management and for the customer. The master schedule gives you a complete picture of the project on a single page.

Each task group should have a separate schedule by itself, i.e., a maximum of about 40 tasks, namely, detailing all the tasks to complete the objectives of that task group. Designing a subassembly, building a second tier assembly, writing a source

Figure 4.1   Typical work breakdown structure for a project.

code, or a subcontractor's detailed schedule can be examples of these task groups. These task groups should be well defined, logical, and bounded efforts with the allocated resources and baselines. As a rule of thumb in a task group, combine tasks that take less than a week to complete. Do not have tasks that last longer than three weeks. If a task lasts more than three weeks, i.e., program coding, break it down to manageable shorter-duration tasks after discussing it with the task owner, so that you can assess the task completeness more accurately.

Discuss and finalize each task's duration, order, and dependencies with its owners. They have to buy in to what they have to achieve and in what time frame. Include an engineering efficiency factor in your schedule. Project-related work efficiency is about 80 to 85 percent. Also, most engineering task owners are overly optimistic about their hour estimates. If a task owner gives you a 40-hour estimate to complete a task, show it as 48 hour in your schedule. Further, learning-curve and training times should be considered and put into the project schedule. Learning-curve and training costs should not be charged to the project but should go into the company's general training overhead bucket. These issues should be discussed with the team member's supervisor, and learning-curve and training costs should be charged appropriately.

Above and beyond work efficiency estimates, international travel time and jet lag inefficiencies should also be added to the task duration. For example, for a trip from the United States to Malaysia, a 24-hour travel time and a 24-hour jet lag recovery time are appropriate.

In some cases, the man hours allocated to a task might be cut by as much as 50 percent in order to be able to be cost competitive in a project. If an engineering task is originally estimated to take 160 hour, and 80 hour is allocated to it in the final cost version of the project, you have to be fair and allocate the task owner the original 160 hour, and work with him closely to see how that task can be completed below 160 hour.

Part-time team members can have conflicting priorities and interests. Their tasks need well-defined scopes, and they need closer follow up. If you get a team member for 20 percent of his or her time, fix a day during the week with the person to work only on your project. Most productive days during the week are Tuesday, Wednesday, and Thursday. Avoid Mondays and Fridays.

Do not forget to include holidays and observances for your domestic and international teams, customer's team, and subcontractors' teams. Also include upcoming and forecasted special events for each team member to your project schedule, i.e., weddings, vacations, maternity leaves, etc.

More often than not, you will not have the final schedules at the beginning of a project from your subcontractors that can go into your overall schedule. In several cases you might not even have the subcontractors finalized and purchase orders released. In these cases, you have to put an estimated duration into your schedule after having discussions with the potential subcontractors. It is not recommended

ID	Task Name	Duration	Start	Finish	2nd Quarter			3rd Quarter			4th Quarter			1st Quarter		
					Apr	May	Jun	Jul	Aug	Sep	Oct	Nov	Dec	Jan	Feb	Mar
1	WO-6215 MERCURY PROJECT	93.33 days	Mon 6/12/06	Mon 10/23/06			▼━━━━━━━━━━━━━━━━━━━━▼									
2	Project Kick-Off Meeting	1 day	Mon 6/12/06	Mon 6/12/06		Team										
3	Design Subsystem A	10 days	Mon 6/13/06	Mon 6/26/06		Designer 1										
4	Design Subsystem B	6 days	Tue 6/13/06	Tue 6/20/06		Designer 2										
5	Design Subsystem C	15 days	Tue 6/13/06	Mon 7/3/06		Designer 3										
6	Submit Customer Interface Drawings	1 day	Wed 7/5/06	Wed 7/5/06		Team										
7	Customer Design Review	2 days	Thu 7/6/06	Fri 7/7/06		Customer, Team										
8	Submit Customer Drawings	0 days	Fri 7/7/06	Fri 7/7/06		7/7										
9	Submit Regulatory Agency Design Package	0 days	Fri 7/7/06	Fri 7/7/06		7/7										
10	Order Materials And Components	30 days	Mon 7/10/06	Fri 8/8/06				Purchasing 1, Purchasing 2								
11	Fabrication Of Parts	45 days	Mon 7/24/06	Mon 9/25/06					Fab 1, Fab 2, Fab 3, Fab 4							
12	All Materials And Components Received	0 days	Tue 9/26/06	Tue 9/26/06						9/26						
13	Assembly Of System	15 days	Thu 9/14/06	Wed 10/4/06						Assy 1, Assy 2, Assy 3						
14	Pre-Testing	5 days	Thu 10/5/06	Wed 10/11/06						TE 1, TE 2						
15	Customer And Regulatory Agency Acceptance Tests	3.33 days	Thu 10/12/06	Tue 10/17/06							Customer, TE 1, TE 2					
16	Packaging And Shipment Of System	3 days	Tue 10/17/06	Fri 10/20/06							Shipping Dept					
17	Project Closure Meeting	1 day	Fri 10/20/06	Mon 10/23/06							Team					

Figure 4.2   Sample MS Project master schedule.

that a task duration estimate be put down for a subcontractor depending upon his past performance because things might have changed considerably since your company dealt with him or her in the past. It might be a longer lead time to get steel from a steel mill due to overwhelming demand. Your favorite precision-machining subcontractor might be going through an equipment upgrade and have a two-week down time right when your task hits his or her doorstep. Your favorite electronic board manufacturer might be saturated by a large order, and his or her lead time might be two months longer.

Here are examples of a project master schedule and a task group schedule (Figure 4.2 and 4.3).

A good practice is to sort these schedules by task owners and give each task owner his or her own schedule for the whole project. It is also a good practice to share a summarized master schedule with your customer and with your upper management. From the initial project schedule, determine all the tasks that are on the critical path. These will need more focus from the project manager and will also need quicker risk management decisions that the other tasks.

Another issue that usually comes up is the sharing of schedules. Most people in your company, at the customer's, or at overseas offices might not have MS Project, or they might have an earlier version. Therefore, they will not be able to open your attached MS Project schedule file. Therefore, always convert the MS Project file to a PDF file and send that to other people who have to see the project schedules.

Make sure that the resources are not overloaded and, at the same time, they are not idle. Idle times will be most likely charged to the project if people do not have

ID	Task Name	Duration	Start	Finish	June				July					August	
					6/4	6/11	6/18	6/25	7/2	7/9	7/16	7/23	7/30	8/6	8/13
1	WO-6215 DESIGN SUBSYSTEM C	15 days	Tue 6/13/06	Mon 7/3/06											
2	Stress Calcs	2 days	Tue 6/13/06	Wed 6/14/06	Designer 3										
3	Fatigue Calcs	2 days	Tue 6/13/06	Wed 6/14/06	Consultant 1										
4	Check Calcs	1 day	Tue 6/15/06	Thu 6/15/06	Checker 1										
5	Assembly Dwg	3 days	Fri 6/16/06	Tue 6/20/06	Designer 3										
6	Component Dwgs 1-9	3 days	Wed 6/21/06	Fri 6/23/06	Designer 3										
7	Check Dwgs	2 days	Mon 6/26/06	Tue 6/27/06	Checker 1										
8	Update Per Checks	0.5 days	Wed 6/26/06	Wed 6/28/06	Designer 3										
9	Back Check	0.5 days	Wed 6/28/06	Wed 6/28/06	Checker 1										
10	Design Review	1 day	Thu 6/29/06	Thu 6/29/06	Involved Team Members, Fab, Assy, QC, Test										
11	Update Dwgs Per Design Review	1 day	Fri 6/30/06	Fri 6/30/06	Designer 3										
12	Document Control Release	1 day	Mon 7/3/06	Mon 7/3/06	Designer 3, Document Control										

Figure 4.3 Sample MS Project task group schedule.

anything else to do. If a team member has an idle period, get that person assigned to another task, get him or her trained, or loan him or her to another project during the idle period. Always include international holidays and task-owner-related other nonworking days that are affecting your project into its schedule.

After the initial layout of the project schedule, check the milestones. See if your team's efforts meet all the customer's contract milestones. Project schedule milestones should agree with the project contract milestones. If you cannot achieve any of the contract milestones, immediately inform the customer and show the customer the reasons why you cannot achieve a certain milestone and request an extension. Make sure the customer agrees on the new milestone date in writing. Also make sure that there are no penalties or liquidated damages involved with the milestone date change.

Typical contract payment milestones for an equipment system design, manufacturing, test, and delivery is given in Figure 4.4. Notice that the first payment milestone is at the submittal of engineering drawings and not at their approval. The difference between a drawings submittal payment versus a drawings approval payment can take as much as four to eight weeks.

Planning for Information Management

Planning for information management is also crucial to an international project. As the project manager, you have to manage the information flow with the customers, team members, subcontractors, regulatory agencies, etc. The information management system should be set up before the project kickoff meetings and explained to all involved parties.

Payment Milestones
• 10% Upon Submittal Of All Required Engineering Drawings Listed In Section 5.1 Of The Specifications • 30% Upon Receipt Of Major Raw Materials and Equipment • 50% Upon Delivery Of Equipment • 10% Upon Submittal Of Final Documentation And Third Party Design & Survey Compliance

Figure 4.4   Typical payment milestones.

All electronic information that is not in document control should be kept in a project folder that is divided into major subfolders. The project folder should be in the company network drive and should be backed up at least daily. It should be protected as a read-only folder. Nobody should be able to delete a file from the project folder without the project manager's written request to the company's IT group.

A subfolder in the project folder should contain all the names, titles, phone numbers (business, cell, and home), fax numbers, e-mail addresses, and mailing addresses of all project team members, customers contacts, major subcontractors contacts, consultants, regulatory agency contacts, etc.

If digital storage of information is not reliable, then a paper folder system should be implemented as a backup divided into major subfolders. The paper documents should be filed chronologically.

For example, all project schedule files should be kept in a schedule subfolder. File names should be descriptive and contain the updated or received date, i.e., "master schedule 8 July 05.mpp." A file should be stored in a specific folder and not in duplicate locations. Duplication of file storage and dimensions or specifications in documents or drawings cause confusion and error. During an engineering change, you will never remember to update all the duplications residing in all the project files.

Only the project manager, or team members in the project manager's presence, should be able to communicate with the customer. Every communication link should have a predetermined backup. For the project manager, the backup can be the contracts manager, or, if there is a dual project manager, namely, one for technical matters and one for business matters, they can back up each other. Communication backups should be assigned for the customers' project managers, subcontractors' project managers, and regulatory agencies' examiners. You should have every communication link's primary and backup person's e-mail address, work phone number, cell phone number, fax number, and even home phone number with their country codes in an accessible folder. You should also know how to dial these phone numbers internationally and within the country.

Some customers require that communication has to be done with a sequential message numbering system. Then you have to create a communication table file for the project that has a sequentially assigned number column along with date, communication originator's name, and the communication title description columns. You have to fill a row of this table to get a new message number automatically. You have to include this message number with the message title in the subject field in your communication with the customer. This is one way of tracking the messages and also referring to them in all communications.

All scope changes, meeting minutes, customers' comments on reviewed documents, subcontractors' comments on reviewed documents, regulatory agency's comments on reviewed documents, project status reports, etc., should be stored in your document control system. They should all go through an official release system according to your document control procedures. A typical list of project management documentation and its control and storage requirements are given in Figure 4.5.

Some documents have to be approved by the customer or by the regulatory agency. Each document sent out of the company should be recorded in an external transmittal form. All documents should be sent out in Adobe Acrobat PDF format unless there are other formats that have been stipulated in the contract agreement. All comments that are received about the particular document should be linked to the engineering change notice and to the document that it is related to. Sometimes the documents and comments go back and forth several times until the document reaches the "Approved Without Comments" stage. All correspondence about a document should be stored in the company document control system in date sequence. Most contracts have response time limits on comments and document submittals, and the typical response time limit is two to four weeks.

All controlled documents regarding the project should go through the project manager's review and approval before their release. You have to assign a backup for this task in case you are out of the office. You do not want document releases to get bogged down and wait for you to return. A document review history for the customer can be tracked by a simple spreadsheet as follows:

Figure 4.6 shows that the document turnaround time was less than two weeks from the project side and from the customer side. In most international projects, such quick document turnaround time from the customer or from subcontractors is a dream come true. You can experience critical documents that got hung up

DOCUMENTATION DESCRIPTION	CONTROL & STORAGE
1. Drawings	Document Control
2. Calculations	Document Control
3. Computer Programs	Document Control
4. Manufacturing Instruction	Document Control
5. Quality Control Procedures	Document Control
6. Test Procedures	Document Control
7. Non-Conformance Reports	Document Control
8. Installation, Operation, & Maintenance Procedures	Document Control
9. Customer Specifications	Document Control
10. Customer Specifications Summary	Document Control
11. Supplier drawings	Document Control
12. Project Status Reports	Document Control
13. All Other Project Required Documents	Document Control
14. Design Review Meetings Reports	Document Control
15. Contact Information	Project Folder
16. Customer Meeting reports	Document Control
17. Customer E-Mail, Telecon, & Videocon Reports	Project Folder
18. Suppliers Meeting Reports	Document Control
19. Suppliers E-Mail, Telecon, & Videocon Reports	Project Folder
20. Internal Team Meeting Reports	Document Control
21. Internal Team E-Mail, Telecon, & Videocon Reports	Project Folder
22. Upper Management Meeting Reports	Document Control
23. Upper Management E-Mail, Telecon, & Videocon Reports	Project Folder
24. Consultants Meeting Reports	Document Control
25. Consultants E-Mail, Telecon, & Videocon Reports	Project Folder
26. Regulatory Agencies Meeting Reports And Certificates	Document Control
27. Regulatory Agency E-Mail, Telecon, & Videocon Reports	Project Folder

Figure 4.5   A typical project management documentation.

Document # & Title	Engr. Change Order #	Transmittal Date	Transmitted By	Document Status
C-014556 Rev. 1 Structural Interface		14 Aug 05	Transmittal Doc # 4335	
Comments On C-014556 Rev. 1		24 Aug 05	E. Starr e-mail	Not Approved
C-014556 Rev. 2 Structural Interface	ECN-8215	4 Sep 05	Transmittal Doc # 4377	
Comments On C-014556 Rev. 2		12 Sep 05	E. Starr e-mail	Proceed With Comments
C-014556 Rev. 3 Structural Interface	ECN-8287	17 Sep 05	Transmittal Doc # 4421	
Comments On C-014556 Rev. 3		27 Sep 05	E. Starr e-mail	Approved Without Comments

Figure 4.6   Document review history tracking spreadsheet.

at a customer's site more than three months and at regulatory agency more than four months during the review process. This can be frustrating to an international project manager, and he or she has to persist with politely putting pressure on his or her customer to get a timely response.

Dates should be standardized so that everyone around the world can understand them and do not get confused by them. It is easy to encounter date and time misunderstandings due to nonstandard and condensed messages. For example, what does this date mean: "4/5/05"? It can be interpreted as 4 May 05 in Europe, or it can be 5 April 05 in the United States. Also, for different time zones, specify your time zone in your message, i.e., 10 a.m. PST (Pacific Standard Time).

For example, a clean teleconference meeting notice to a subcontractor can be as follows:

Teleconference initiator: ABC Design Corporation, San Jose, California, USA, for ABC PO # 586395—Mercury Project Load Cells Weekly Status Meeting
Initiating Person: Raj Patel—Mercury Project Manager
Initiating Phone Number: 1-405-867-1543
Date: 4 May 2007 Friday
Time: 10 AM PST (Pacific Standard Time)
Attendees: Raj Patel—Mercury Project Manager, Jim Knox—Design Engineer, and Peter Summers—Purchasing Agent
Teleconference Receiver: Load Cell, Inc., Buffalo, New York, USA
Receiving Person: Tim North—Project Manager
Receiving Phone Number: 1-716-528-0124
Date: 4 May 2007 Friday
Time: 1 PM EST (Eastern Standard Time)

Attendees: Tim North—Project Manager, and Russ Blue—Design Engineer
Teleconference Duration: 1 hour
Agenda:
    Load Cell Cover Interference—10 minutes
    Load Cell Cable Size and Routing—15 Minutes
    Regulatory Agency Design Certification Status—5 Minutes
    Calibration Procedure—10 Minutes
    Packaging and Shipment Process—5 Minutes
    Other Issues—10 Minutes
    Action Items—5 Minutes

The information management system should also include the times for your recurring meetings with your domestic team, international teams, customers, regulatory agency, and major subcontractors. For example, every Monday at 4 p.m. PST, there will be a general domestic team meeting in Conference Room # 2. Every Tuesday at 4 p.m. PST (9 a.m. Malaysian Standard Time), there will be a general Malaysian team videoconference in Videoconference Room # 1. There will be a teleconference with the customer every Friday at 7 a.m. PST (3 p.m. London time) in Conference Room # 5.

Once you have the project specifications and standards summary, project work breakdown structure, project schedule, and project information management system ready, you can start holding the project kickoff meetings.

Kickoff Meetings

Before the project kickoff meeting with the customer, list all the open issues, specifications and standards clarifications, gray areas, challenging areas, and critical path tasks. Prepare a detailed agenda for the meeting. Discuss every item in detail. Make sure all the communication links and backups are determined on both sides. Mostly technical and nontechnical (i.e., sales, purchasing or contracts) communication links are separate. Record all the agenda items, conclusions reached, and action items, their owners, and due dates. Make sure that the meeting minutes are read and approved by the customer.

In international meetings, put the flags of the countries involved at the center of the conference table. If translations are needed, arrange for a translator to be present. Prepare some events such as dinners and shows that represent your culture to the customer. Make sure that the customer has adequate and private offices or conference rooms during these meetings. Make sure that they have all the communication devices such as telephones, Internet connections, cell phones, etc., during their visit. They should also have access to a computer printer. Always consider their jet lag and trip fatigue, and adjust the meeting durations accordingly.

For example, one of the customer's representative's (from England) cell phone charger is not working. In such a case, you can assign someone to go out, search, and find a special cell phone charger for him, or you might do this yourself. A $15 charger can make him very happy. If the customer wants to pay for the charger, you should tell him that it is a small memento from your company, and do not accept his payment offer. During the departure exchanges, give the customer's representatives small souvenirs that represent your company and the city you are in.

Project teams kickoff meetings, domestic and international, should cover the deliverables, tough-to-achieve and unique specifications and standards, critical-path tasks, major subcontractors that are being considered, contract penalties, unique contract obligations, regulatory agency design and test certification requirements, unit requirements for all documents, multiple language requirements for all documents, project utility requirements, project environmental requirements, etc. You should explain in detail to the team who is responsible for what task. Make sure that all the team members and production planning, contracts, and sales people attend the initial team kickoff meeting. Then let the owner of each task explain his or her responsibilities, critical specifications, schedule, and deliverables for the project. Provide work breakdown structure, charge numbers, and information management and communications specifics.

Kickoff meetings with other departments can be with an individual department or a group of departments, depending upon how extensive the interdepartmental link requirements are for the project. For example, if all the nonstandard purchased items have to be source inspected by the company quality group, regulatory agency inspectors, and the customer, you better bring the quality group and the purchasing group together to a kickoff meeting to highlight their responsibilities and interactions.

If there is a specific electronic file transfer protocol (FTP) to the customer, bring in your IT department to explain their procedures to your team. If there are security requirements in dealing with customer's documents, bring in your document control department to explain the document security procedures to your team.

Group meetings between departments are informative and interactive but inefficient. Several people wait around for their turn to come, and do not care for other discussions. To get around this inefficiency, some groups from your team or from other departments might be on call to the meeting and are invited in when their turn comes up.

Subcontractors' kickoff meetings should be, if possible, at the subcontractors' sites. Their operations, people, organizational structure, and role of project manager for your project should be fully understood. Again, all the specifications related to the subcontractor have to be clear. All the deliverables and their timelines have to be understood. Tests and acceptance criteria have to be ironed out. All communication channels have to be clearly laid out. It is always advisable not to have multiple communication channels; things get dropped and fall through the cracks.

As a project manager, you have to evaluate the risk factor of every subcontractor. Should a weekly status teleconference be sufficient with this subcontractor? Should you send someone every other week to their plant to assess their progress? Should you have a vendor engineer implanted continuously into their operations? How stable are their people? Can you trust your counterpart at this subcontractor? What is the subcontractor's quality and delivery record in the past? Is the subcontractor overloaded with other work and unable to pull off your job on time? All these questions and their answers will make you decide as to how to deal with the risk factors involving every major subcontractor for the project.

Also, kickoff meetings with the domestic and international sites' upper managements are a must. Make sure all the upper managers who are involved with the project are in attendance. Sometimes it is hard to get every upper manager into a meeting room at a specified time. In such cases, do not delay the kickoff meeting if you have a quorum. You should always discuss the kickoff meeting minutes later with the missing upper managers. During the upper management kickoff meeting, all the risky areas of the project should be put on the table and discussed in detail with proposed solutions.

It is highly recommended that minutes for critical meetings be kept in a standard format and as a controlled document. Critical meeting examples are customer kickoff, domestic and international teams kickoff, kickoff with other departments, kickoff with significant subcontractors, kickoff with domestic and international upper managements, customers' project reviews, subcontractors' project reviews, project design reviews, upper management project reviews, and regulatory agency design reviews.

Monitoring Schedule and Cost Performances

Another important factor in project planning is how to monitor schedule and cost performances. As the project manager, you have to agree with the accounting department on the work breakdown structure and the cost buckets. If you can set up the costing system in a way that all costs to your project, including the time card hourly charges, can be approved by you before they go into the project buckets, that would be best. The object is not to be a control freak but to prevent the many mistakes made in charges that go into project cost buckets intentionally or unintentionally.

During the planning phase of the project, prepare an earned-value spreadsheet that covers the major task groups, subcontractors, and purchases. An excellent reference book is *Earned Value Project Management* by Quentin W. Fleming and Joel M. Koppelman.

You have to update these project schedule and cost analyses monthly and present them to upper management. Also, two metrics—schedule performance index and cost performance index—will give you a good indication of how you are doing

BCWS=Budgeted Cost Of Work Scheduled	SPI=Schedule Performance Index=BCWP/BCWS
BCWP=Budgeted Cost Of Work Performed	CPI=Cost Performance Index=BCWP/ACWP
ACWP=Actual Cost Of Work Performed	EAC=ACWP+(BAC-BCWP)

Tasks	4 Weeks BCWS, k$	8 Weeks BCWS, k$	12 Weeks BCWS, k$	16 Weeks BCWS, k$	20 Weeks BCWS, k$	24 Weeks BCWS, k$	BAC, BUDGET @ COMPLETION TOTALS, k$	EAC, ESTIMATE @ COMPLETION TOTALS, k$
Design A	32	16					48	52.4
Build A			50	50			100	100
Test A					32		32	32
Spec B	16						16	20
Purchase B		25	25	50			100	100
Test B					25		25	25
Integrate A & B						32	32	32
Total Project	48	41	75	100	57	32	353	361.4

Project Status Date: 4 weeks after Project start date

Tasks	4 Weeks BCWS, k$	Work Completion Estimates 4 Weeks % Work Complete	Costs From Accounting 4 Weeks ACWP, k$	4 Weeks BCWP, k$	4 Weeks SPI<1 Behind Schedule	4 Weeks CPI<1 Over Budget	4 Weeks Schedule Variance, days
Design A	32	80	30	25.6	0.80	0.85	-4
Build A							
Test A							
Spec B	16	100	20	16	1.00	0.80	0
Purchase B							
Test B							
Integrate A & B							
Total Project	48	12	50	41.6	0.87	0.83	-2.7

Figure 4.7 Typical earned-value spreadsheet.

schedulewise and costwise at a certain cutoff point in the project. A typical earned-value spreadsheet is given in Figure 4.7 for a 24-week project. Also in Figure 4.7, schedule and cost performances are evaluated after four weeks into the project.

There are two critical inputs to this spreadsheet that you have to gather from your task groups and from your accounting department for project evaluation. In the earned-value spreadsheet example given in Figure 4.7, after four weeks of execution for a 24-week project, 12 percent of the budgeted work is completed. The project is falling behind schedule, is over budget, and the cost estimate at completion is 2.4 percent, [(361.4 − 353) × 100/353], over budget.

First inputs are the percentage work completion estimates for each task. Mutually determine the percentage work completion estimate with the task owner after discussing the remaining duties left for completion. Beware that task owners always tend to overestimate their percentage work completions. From these percentage work completion estimates, MS Project will calculate the budgeted cost of work performed (BCWP), which is the earned value for that task group. Once you divide this earned value with the budgeted cost of work scheduled (BCWS), which is the planned value for that task group up to the evaluation date, you will get the schedule performance index (SPI) for that task group.

SPI < 1 means the work for the task group is behind schedule.

SPI = 1 means the work for the task group is 100 percent complete.

The second input, namely, the actual cost for each task group, is obtained from the accounting department. The key is to have all the costs inputted into the cost bucket by the accounting department in a timely fashion. There is always a lag time up to a couple of weeks before all the costs go into a project cost bucket. Your actual project evaluation date may be 31 May, but the cost inputs in the accounting department may have been completed up to 21 May. You have to wait a week or two to get the cost inputs completed up to 31 May to be able to have an accurate cost performance index (CPI) for the task group in question. You have to push the accounting department to minimize this lag time.

Always check the actual cost numbers for errors. Do not get charged for someone's time if he or she did not contribute to your project. Do not get charged for an equipment that does not belong to your project. Believe it or not, these wrong charges occur.

The dollar number you get for the task group through 31 May is called the actual cost of work performed (ACWP). Once you divide BCWP by ACWP, you get CPI, which is the ratio of earned value to actual cost up to the project evaluation date.

CPI < 1 means you have a cost overrun for that task group up to the project evaluation date.

CPI > 1 means you are under budget for that task group up to the project evaluation date.

It is tough to estimate percentage of work completions, namely, the earned values, in software development tasks, design calculations tasks, or similar tasks where the completed and leftover portions of a task are subjective. To get your arms around these subjective tasks, break down the task to smaller and accountable subtasks with the owner of the task. These indicators will give you an idea about the task groups that are in trouble. You have to take decisive steps to remedy the issues immediately and present the corrective actions to upper management for approval. You as the project manager should present these schedule and cost performance indices to your upper management monthly or in the event of an emergency. You should also bring suggested solutions for the poor performing task groups and discuss them in detail with upper management and get their buy-in to proceed in a new direction.

Poor schedule performance can be fixed by adding more resources or by working overtime or by changing team members, or by shipping airfreight instead of sea freight, etc. However, it is hard to remedy poor cost performance. It might be that the task group's budgeted cost was underestimated to begin with. There might be cost overruns due to inflation, international monetary parity fluctuations, or a nonperforming subcontractor. Sometimes a cost overrun in one task group can be offset by an underbudget performance in another. Overall cost overruns and underruns can balance each other out. You are a very lucky project manager if this cost balancing occurs. Cost overruns should be discussed in detail with upper management at least once a month. You should get permission from upper management to pick into the project contingency funds, if there are any, in your budget, or lower the expected margin projections for the project.

Every project does not start with the required planning that was outlined in this chapter. Sometimes you start your project with missing team members. For example, a new hire might be starting in two weeks, and he or she will be a member of your team. A Korean engineer from your division in Korea has joined your team, but his visa formalities for entry into the United States have not been completed. Another example is that an engineering specialist, in dynamic finite element analysis (FEA), is finishing another project and will be available to you in a month. On the specifications side, the salesperson and the customer put the initial project specifications on the back of a napkin during their negotiations dinner and you have to start from this napkin. You could not agree with your accounting department on the project work breakdown structure and charge numbers. The people working on the project started to charge to the wrong cost buckets. The customer's project manager is in Norway and he is trying to complete another project, and he will not be available for a project kickoff meeting for another three weeks. Your document control and the customer's document control cannot connect through the Internet yet, though your people are scheduled to be trained on the customer's document control system in the next two weeks. These are some examples of the bumps that can occur at the beginning of a project. Your job is to get over these bumps as quickly as possible or find alternate routes and start the project on a sound footing.

Checklist for Chapter 4

- How much time do you have to plan and launch the project?
- Do you have a plan for yourself as to how to complete all the project kickoff requirements?

Selecting Team Members

- Have a definite say in forming the domestic and international project teams.
- Interview every domestic and international team member face to face or with videoconferencing. Last resort is a telephone interview.
- Minimize the number of part-time team members.
- Do not forget to include team members' training durations into your schedule.
- How proficient in English are the international team members?
- Do you need translators for your project?
- Include travel durations and time lost due to jet lag into your planning.
- Include team members' special time-offs into your planning.
- Include your customer's and subcontractors' time-offs into your planning.
- Do you know the strengths and weaknesses of each team member?
- Do you have a balanced team in regard to experience for the project that your are going to tackle?
- Can you form subteams for mentoring?
- Can the team members that will join the project later still contribute to the project? Can you juggle their tasks so that project milestones can still be met?
- Did you agree with every team member's supervisor regarding your contribution to performance reviews?
- Do you know in detail all the differences in review criteria in different divisions of your company and in the international sites that affect your project?
- Have you rejected team members who can degrade team harmony and morale?
- Do you have to have outside consultants and contractors on your project team?
- Have you interviewed the potential outside consultants and contractors in detail?
- Are you going to assign outside consultants and contractors well-defined and easy-to-track tasks?
- Will the outside consultants and contractors use the same design tools and revision levels as your company's while executing their project tasks?
- Are you taking on the project in the middle? Have you made the necessary adjustments to the team members? Have you corrected the issues that are damaging the project's progress?

Creating a Summary of Project Specifications and Standards

- Are all the project specifications and standards in the English language?
- Do you need experts in certain fields to summarize the specifications or standards? Have you outlined the areas you will need technical help in?
- Have you prepared a summary of project specifications?
- Have you prepared a summary of project standards?
- Is the summary of project specifications and standards a controlled document?

- Do all the specifications and standards listed in your summary have revision levels and specify the sections that apply to your project?
- Does the summary have customer's scope of supply with delivery dates, late penalties, and early delivery rewards?
- Does the summary list the required regulatory agency design and test certificates?
- Does the summary cover the hierarchy of specifications and standards?
- Does the summary have the project name, proposal identifier, work breakdown structure, charge numbers, major subcontractors, consultants, and domestic and international team members with their responsibilities?
- Specify applicable units in your project specifications summary.
- Specify applicable languages in your project specifications summary.
- Specify spares requirements in your project specifications summary.
- Specify design review requirements in your project specifications summary.
- Summarize specifications for each deliverable item separately.
- Summarize design review and design calculation requirements for each deliverable item separately.
- Specify all special requirements that are needed for the designers such as interface, environmental, utility, materials, fabrication, coating, acceptance tests, inspections, documentation, and shipping.
- Include similar historical projects and lessons learned from these past projects into your summary.
- Are all the gray areas regarding the project specifications and standards cleared with the customer?
- Did you get the summary specifications and standards reviewed by company management and by international project sites leaders?
- Did you get the project summary specifications and standards document released as revision 1 before the kickoff meetings?

Creating Work Breakdown Structure

- Is the work breakdown structure a mirror image of the project deliverables?
- Is the project management a separate cost bucket in the work breakdown structure?
- Are the cost buckets broken down into logical subsets such as design, check, design review, manufacturing, test, travel, etc.?
- Are you in agreement with your financial department regarding the project work breakdown structure, cost buckets, and charge numbers?
- Are you going to be on the approval route for all the charges to your project?
- Agree with your financial department on a lag time after which the actual project costs will be available to you for project status evaluations.
- Make sure that all the domestic and international team members know the appropriate project charge numbers.

Creating the Initial Schedule

- Do you have a project scheduler helping you?
- Are you going to have one schedule for the whole project, or are you going to break the project schedule up into task groups?
- Are you going to create a master schedule with milestones, task groups, and dependencies on a single page for upper management and for your customer?
- Discuss each task group's tasks and their durations with its owners before putting them on to the schedule.
- Do you have a task duration less than a week in a task group schedule? If possible, combine tasks that are less than a week with other tasks unless they are significant ones such as design reviews, acceptance tests, etc.
- Do not have a task duration longer than three weeks in a task group schedule. Break it up into segments where each subtask completion can be verified objectively.
- Have you included a task efficiency factor into the task duration estimates?
- Have you included learning-curve and training factors into the task duration estimates?
- Have you included international travel times and jet leg inefficiencies into the task duration estimates?
- Are you charging learning-curve and training costs to the company training cost bucket instead of to the project?
- Are there any man-hours cut during the negotiations process to reduce the bid cost of the project? How are you dealing with these shortchanged tasks? Are you allocating them the normal hours it will take to complete them?
- Have you included all the domestic and international holidays and observances for your team members in your schedule?
- Have you included all the domestic and international holidays and observances for your customers' team members in your schedule?
- Have you included all the domestic and international holidays and observances for your subcontractors' team members in your schedule?
- Have you included each team member's special time-offs in your schedule?
- If you do not have all the delivery dates from your subcontractors, how are you estimating these unknown tasks' durations? Are you getting fresh delivery estimates from each subcontractor, or are you relying on their historical performances?
- Will you be able to share your project schedule outputs with everyone involved around the world? Do you have to change your output format?
- Are there overloaded resources? Have you smoothed out their overloads?
- Are there idle resources? Have you discussed these idle times with their owners? How are they going to utilize their idle times?
- Does your schedule match with all the project agreement milestones?

- Have you sorted the schedules by task owners and provided each team member his or her own schedule?
- Have you determined all the tasks that are on the critical path? Have you informed critical-path task owners about the consequences of delaying their tasks?
- It is advisable to have a frozen project schedule file for each workweek. Any updates that are made during a workweek should go to next workweek's schedule.

Planning for Information Management

- Set up a complete information management system for the project so that all team members, both domestic and international, can use it effectively.
- Identify as to what documents will go through the company's document control system.
- Can your international project sites access your document control system?
- Who are the approvers and their backups for different types of project documents that will go into the company's document control system.
- Identify as to what documents will go into the project folders and subfolders in the company network.
- How are the project folders protected? No one should be able to delete any of the files in the project folder.
- How are you assuring that duplicate files are not stored in separate project subfolders?
- Is all the worldwide project contacts information in a project subfolder?
- Is your electronic filing system reliable? Is it backed up daily?
- Can your international project sites access your network files?
- Do you need a paper folder system as a backup?
- Does every communication link have a backup? Are the communication links reliable? Do they have excessive downtime? What are the communication alternatives in case of downtime?
- Are there special requirements in communicating with the customer, i.e., sequential numbering of each message?
- Do customers' communications links have backups?
- Do your subcontractors' communication links have backups?
- Do the project regulatory agencies' communication links have backups?
- Prepare a project management documents list with document description and document control and project folder storage requirements.
- What are the document transmittal procedures to your customer?
- What are the document transmittal procedures to your subcontractors?
- What are the document transmittal procedures to regulatory agencies?
- Prepare a document review history tracking spreadsheet for the customer.

- Emphasize the communication date format to your team members.
- Make a table of recurring meetings for the project and distribute them to involved parties. These recurring meetings should cover domestic team meetings, international team meetings, customer meetings, and major subcontractor meetings.

Kickoff Meeting with Customer

- Prepare for a kickoff meeting with the customer. List all the open issues with the customer. List all required clarifications for specifications and standards. List all gray areas in the contract. List all the challenging areas in the contract. List the critical path tasks. List all required clarifications for the interfaces.
- Does the customer agree to the meeting schedule and agenda before the meeting?
- Is there a translator requirement during the meeting?
- Are the customer's needs such as lunches, dinners, private offices, communications devices, etc., taken care of?
- Have you considered your customer's jet lag and trip fatigue and adjusted the meetings and other activities accordingly?
- Have you covered all the open issues regarding the project? Have you recorded the decisions made during the meeting?
- Have you covered project documentation, documentation security, and electronic file transfer requirements?
- Have you recorded all the action items, their owners, and their due dates?
- Have you agreed on the communication channels with their backups?
- Have you arranged for the customer to approve the meeting minute before leaving?
- Have you released the customer kickoff meeting minutes in your document control system and sent copies to all the attendees?

Kickoff Meetings with Domestic and International Team Members

- Prepare for the kickoff meeting with the team members. If time zones do not allow a single meeting, have several kickoff meetings. Invite production planning, contracts, and sales to the initial kickoff meeting.
- Cover who the customer is and what the overall project is about. Cover all customer's contacts, both technical and nontechnical.
- Provide everyone a copy of specifications and standards summary.
- Cover who is responsible for what task.
- Cover tough-to-achieve and unique specifications and standards.
- Cover major subcontractors.

- Cover contract penalties and rewards and unique contract obligations.
- Cover all the regulatory agency design and test certification requirements.
- Cover project unit requirements.
- Cover project language requirements.
- Cover project utility and environmental requirements.
- Cover project documentation, documentation security, and electronic file transfer requirements.
- Give a detailed overview of the project internal name, work breakdown structure, and charge accounts.
- Give a detailed overview of the information management and communication procedures.
- Give a detailed overview of IP and confidentiality requirements.
- Owners of each task group should explain his or her responsibilities, critical specifications, schedule, risk areas, and deliverables.
- Have you released the project team kickoff meeting minutes in your document control system and sent copies to all the attendees?

Kickoff Meetings with Other Departments

- Prepare for kickoff meetings with other departments.
- Meet with each department separately to make the meetings more efficient.
- The department head and people involved with your project in that department should attend the meeting.
- Go over every task, deliverables, task period, and task duration that they will be involved within your project.
- Give a detailed overview of IP and confidentiality requirements.
- Have you released the particular department kickoff meeting minutes in your document control system and sent copies to all the attendees?

Kickoff Meetings with Major Subcontractors

- Prepare for kickoff meetings with major subcontractors.
- Meet with each subcontractor separately at his site.
- Is the subcontractor's organizational structure clear?
- Is the communication channel with backups identified?
- Are all the specifications that apply to the particular subcontractor clear?
- Are the regulatory agency design and test certification requirements clear?
- Cover project documentation, documentation security, and electronic file transfer requirements.
- Have you discussed all the tests and acceptance criteria?
- Have you discussed your customer's involvement with the subcontractor? When will the customer's visits occur? Who is going to coordinate these visits?

- Have you assessed the risk factor regarding this subcontractor?
- How are you going to monitor the progress of this major subcontractor?
- Give a detailed overview of the related IP and confidentiality requirements to this subcontractor.
- Have you released the kickoff meeting minutes with this particular subcontractor in your document control system and sent copies to all the attendees?

Kickoff Meetings with Upper Management

- Prepare for the kickoff meeting with upper management, both domestic and international.
- Discuss risky areas of the project.
- Present solutions for the risky areas and get their inputs.
- Present project master schedule.
- Present schedule performance index procedure.
- Present cost performance index procedure.
- Summarize regulatory agency design and test certificate requirements.
- Give an overview of project IP and confidentiality requirements.
- Give an overview of project documentation, documentation security, and electronic file transfer requirements.
- Release the kickoff meeting minutes with upper management in your document control system and send copies to all the attendees.

Monitoring Schedule and Cost Performances

- Prepare an earned-value spreadsheet to monitor the schedule and cost performance of your project.
- Evaluate the schedule and cost performance of each task at least once a month for a year-long project.
- Obtain a realistic percentage of work completed from each task owner to update your earned-value spreadsheet.
- If the work completion estimates are too subjective, break down the task with its owner into accountable and more objective subtasks.
- Obtain costs incurred in project cost buckets from your financial department up to the project evaluation cutoff point. Make sure that all the costs are valid.
- Calculate schedule and cost performance indices for each task.
- Determine tasks that are in trouble.
- Discuss the troubled tasks with their owners. Prepare options and actions for recovery.
- Present the poorly performing tasks to upper management with options and actions for recovery without any delay.

- If poorly performing tasks are offshore, go there or send there reliable senior people who can help and recover the situation without any delay.
- Record all the bumps you have encountered personnelwise, customerwise, and subcontractorwise during the start of the project and inform your upper management with proposed solutions without any delay.

Chapter 5

Executing an International Project

An international project execution starts with leading the team, which includes leading the domestic team members, international team members, team contractors, customers' teams, subcontractors' teams, regulatory agencies' teams, and the upper management. Nothing of significance happens without the knowledge of the project manager. The project manager has to be on top of every issue. Everyone related to the project comes to the project leader without any reservations to discuss project-related issues. You have to work harder than anyone in the team, solve team members' issues, perform all the project management tasks and, at the same time, keep the team morale high by praising, encouraging, and smiling all the time.

Team Management

Remote controlling international project teams can be very stressful and time consuming. Despite tremendous advances in communication through e-mail, video conferencing, and teleconferencing, there is nothing to beat the face-to-face reality check. If you get the slightest indication that things are not moving forward the way they should, you or someone else designated by you should hop on a plane and go for a face-to-face reality check. If you sense some weakness in offshore team members, you should send a senior engineer to support the offshore team until the task is completed.

For an international project manager, individual team member meetings are more productive as compared to team meetings. Periodic one-on-one meetings with every domestic team member, and with international team leaders, is very effective. The meeting frequency should be decided by you depending upon several factors such as the criticality of the task, experience of the task owner or international team leader, organizational skills of the task owner or the international team leader, schedule performance index for the task, and the cost-performance index. One-on-one domestic meetings should be held in the task owner's office. Periodic meetings with international team leaders can be by videoconferencing or by teleconferencing. It is also advisable to have face-to-face on-site meetings with the international teams at least every two months. Some team members, especially novices, might require a daily ten- or fifteen-minute get together to go over his or her tasks for the day and find solutions to the difficulties he or she is encountering. Some team members might require a once-a-week get-together. These are the more organized and experienced team members who will progress in their tasks without much guidance.

If you have outside consultants and contractors helping you, you should periodically meet with them face-to-face or virtually. The meeting frequency should be determined at the beginning of the project by you depending upon the criticality of the tasks and the risks involved.

Having project team meetings are also important to domestic and international teams' morale and cross-functional information flow. If possible, connecting international project teams to domestic team meetings brings unity to the overall project team. Having team meetings every two or three weeks and at significant events such as kickoff, pre-customer visit, a major issue, successful completion of a project, etc., are recommended.

The team members see the project manager as a problem solver and helper. They trust you and have such confidence in you that they will do whatever they need to solve their issues. The team members' respect for the project manager goes beyond the project to their personal issues. However, you have to keep a distance with the team members in order not to bias your decisions. The following cases are examples from international team members' issues.

An equipment designer and manufacturer in the United States had a large project for a British customer. For equipment training and installation, an experienced engineer was sent to the United Kingdom. The engineer's stay in the United Kingdom was estimated to be two months. This U.S. company had a policy about expenses such that they gave you a credit card in your name. The credit card owner was responsible for paying the monthly credit card balance. The company reimbursed an expense report within two weeks after receipt of the expense report supported by receipts. The experienced engineer piled up expenses in the United Kingdom but got heavily involved with his work and could not file an expense report on time. When the time came to pay the monthly credit card balance, the engineer did not have enough funds to cover the full payment. He called his project manager and asked for help. The project manager immediately took the situation into his hands and discussed it with the finance department and the upper management to make an exception and make an advance payment to the engineer's bank account so that he could cover the credit card payment. The engineer was elated. He did not have to get stressed over his finances. Instead, he focused on his tasks and finished his assignments with flying colors.

A California company in the magnetic recording head industry set up a project to crack the Japanese disk-drive market and become an OEM supplier to several prominent Japanese disk-drive manufacturers. The company team was composed of two Japanese engineers stationed in Japan, two U.S. engineers, and a U.S. engineering project manager stationed in California. All the magnetic recording head developments and manufacturing for product qualification for the company were done in California. Also, the Japanese engineers were trained in California for this team's tasks.

During a trip to Japan, one of the Japanese engineers, Goto'san, said he was getting married in two weeks and invited the project manager and the two U.S. engineers to attend his wedding. He also asked the project manager to be the guest of honor and give the keynote speech during the wedding ceremonies. The project manager and the U.S. engineers accepted the invitation as an honor and set off to prepare for the event.

At the beginning of the project, all three U.S.-based team members took lessons in Japanese language for business people and learned etiquettes of business introductions and meeting protocols as a project preparation requirement. It was very difficult to crack open the OEM door for a U.S. company in Japan, and especially in the data storage industry. Therefore, the protocol during customer interaction had to be perfect.

The tasks for the wedding preparation were very detailed and overwhelming but very gratifying. The right outfit to wear, to learn the do's and don'ts during the wedding ceremonies, what to say in the speech, mixing of Japanese phrases at the beginning and at the end of the speech, when to pause for the translator, the appropriate gift for the couple, etc., were thought out to the utmost detail and were executed without a glitch.

Goto'san and his bride were extremely happy with the event. As a tradition, they also presented all the guests with gifts. After the honeymoon, this Japanese engineer gave an outstanding performance in the team. His hard and smart work made the company crack the door open for four OEM customers in Japan in one year. When operating in a foreign country, learning their customs and respecting their traditions go a long way. It is the duty of the project manager to learn these customs and traditions, pass them on to the team members, and bring unity into the team.

Another matter of cultural understanding and behavior deals with after-work dinner and outings. For example, Japanese engineers work very hard and, after work, they like to go out to eat and drink as a team. You work until 10 p.m. and than go out to dinner and drinks until 1 a.m. Then the Japanese engineers go to their homes, which are at least two hours away, and come back to work at 9 a.m.

This can be a very demanding schedule and might hamper the project's progress. You, as the project manager, might schedule these outings to correspond to a major successful milestone and have them on Fridays.

Another cultural example that might take you by surprise is shaking hands with female engineers in Malaysia. Some Malaysian female engineers do not allow shaking hands with someone outside their families. You have to respect their religious and cultural beliefs and traditions and behave accordingly. Some blunders might jeopardize the progress of the project. Therefore, it is best to learn the do's and don'ts of a culture before you go to that country, and pass on these tips to your team members.

An eyeopening cultural example that also might take you by surprise is the discussion of salaries and bonuses with your colleagues in a foreign country. The salary and bonus questions always come up in a friendly discussion. In countries such as India or Bulgaria, an engineer might be making a tenth of what you are making in the United States. Discussing the salary and bonus issues might cause jealousy and animosity and affect the progress of the project. If such a question is asked, it is better to emphasize the company policy that forbids discussing salary and bonus issues with actual numbers.

The drive for work also varies from country to country. If you are racing to meet a deadline, you might find a Japanese engineer spending days in the office wearing the same clothes and sleeping on a cot to finish his task. In the United States you might experience your team members working 16 hour days to meet a deadline. You will not see the same kind of dedication to work in other countries, especially as you get to warmer climates. It is sometimes called the latitude versus attitude-towards-work syndrome. The meaning of a Japanese minute is quite different from that of a Mexican minute.

During an international project execution, you have to watch and be cognizant of the pressures on your team members and your international teams. Some people can take pressure, but most people buckle under pressure and get burned out. As a project manager, you act as the pressure relief valve by helping your team members or by getting them the necessary support. This smoothing out of pressure improves their performance and enhances dedication to the project objectives.

For example, during a ground-up automated and pneumatic wheelchair lift design for a passenger bus, the designer was having difficulty in smoothing out the motion of the lift under load during prototype testing. He was putting in long hours with no solution in sight. An expert in pneumatic designs was found and brought in as a consultant immediately. The designer and the consultant worked for several days together and changed the necessary valves and the holes to make the system work. Such pressure-relieving actions happen quite often both domestically and internationally during the execution of a project.

During an international project execution, response time is very crucial for good team management. Even if you do not have an answer to a request from a team member, respond immediately by acknowledging the issue and listing the actions you are taking to find a solution, and providing a definite response date. Understand the facts and take the necessary steps to remedy the issue. Fast response time increases everyone's confidence in you as the project leader.

During the execution phase of the project, another unpleasant but significant job of an international project manager is to deal with nonperforming team members and with those who disrupt the team harmony and synergy. Fast action by bringing in upper management and human resources is recommended. If the rabble-rouser is someone you must have for that particular project task, then you have to separate him from the team and deal with him one-on-one.

For example, in an advanced magnetic recording head design project, the project manager had an Ivy League physics Ph.D. in the team who was responsible for the magnetic design of the head. He never said "good morning" to anyone. He never came to team meetings. Above all, he was the prima donna gossiper among team members. He degraded team unity, but the project manager needed his expertise and knowledge during the project. So he decided to deal with the physicist one-on-one and asked him not to interfere with other team member's work. The project manager also brought up the issue with his supervisor and with human resources. The physicist worked in artificial isolation and was let go after the completion of the project.

If you are a good team manager, you would know it from the indications you get from your domestic and international team members if they want to be on your next project team and work with you under any circumstances.

Customer Management

During the execution of an international project, meeting customer's milestones and getting milestone payments for your company should be top priority. However, customer requests, demands, interferences, scope changes, and personnel changes have to be managed carefully so as to be able to meet deliverable and payment milestones.

Customers' main technical and nontechnical contacts and their backups should be fixed from the start of the project. No one in your company should respond to the customer except you or your backup person. Again, response time is very crucial for good customer management. Even if you do not have an answer to a request from your customer, respond immediately by acknowledging the issue on hand listing the actions you are taking to find a solution, and by providing a definite response date. All communication with the customer should be electronically filed in chronological order.

Customer's response to your requests can be more challenging. After all, they are the customers. Sometimes you might get the cold shoulder. As the international project manager, you cannot pester your customer constantly, but a right amount of persistency pays off. Sometimes you might have to help them get an answer.

For example, a British customer could not provide the project manager with the interface structure tolerances in a timely fashion for the subsystem design. The customer's designer was on a month's medical leave, and did not have anyone else to help him. The project manager offered the customer that he himself would do the tolerance stack-up study and send it to the customer for checking and approval so that the subsystem design would not stall.

Scope changes are also a significant portion of project execution. Changes proposed by the customer to specifications, standards, or deliverables have to be evaluated carefully. Effects of the proposed changes to deliverables, the project team, subcontractors, and regulatory agencies can be overwhelming. Major scope changes should go through the official approval routes in your company and the customers' companies. Minor scope changes can be dealt between project managers to make matters expeditious.

In several offshore oil subsystem projects, major scope changes were agreed upon in a written format with the customer's project and purchasing managers, and the official change order was received by the project manager's company several months later due to bureaucratic holdups at the customer's office.

In a technical specification change proposal in the middle of a project, an international customer wanted to increase the loading capacity of the equipment due to a change in their system design requirement. Their scientists claimed that equipment design methods were too conservative. The customer performed its own detailed nonlinear finite element analysis on the equipment and showed that the designed in loading capacity could be increased to the new specification without exceeding the material stress limits in stress-concentrated regions. After reviewing their calculations in detail and after hours of discussions with the customer, it was agreed that the loading capacity of the designed equipment be increased without warranty.

There are occasions when a customer puts a hold on a project or cancels in the middle due to changes in specifications or in-market forces. Your company might put a hold on a project because the customer has missed a milestone payment. Closing out a project under such unusual circumstances can be tricky. You cannot charge to the project anymore, but you have to honor the deliverables up to that point in time. The customer may lose interest in the project, but you still are the project manager and have to wrap things up.

Sometimes tables will be turned and you will propose changes to your customers to make some specifications and standards more doable or to delay milestones and deliverables. Again, major scope changes should go through the official approval routes in your company and the customers' companies, and minor scope changes can be dealt between project managers.

Project status reports to the customer should be bimonthly or monthly. These reports should follow the customer's format, that is, in a way the customer likes to see the report structured. If a project issue is being outlined in the status report, it should also include the proposed solutions. Both should first be discussed with the customer's project manager and, after mutual agreement, should be put into the project status report. The project status reports could be seen by several of the customer's higher managers, and you do not want to create unnecessary stir and commotion regarding your project.

A German customer on a data communication module design project wanted daily status reports. They were adamant about the daily status reporting requirements. After negotiations during the project kickoff meeting, it was agreed to have daily teleconference for status reporting between the project managers. It was also agreed that team members would be called into the teleconference on an as-needed basis.

Status reporting should also come in the other direction, namely, from the customer to you. If you are a subcontractor in a large project, you should get overall project status from your customer at least monthly during your videoconferences or teleconferences. You should put this item into your meeting agenda so that the customer sees it and prepares for it.

Customers' visits to your company or international project sites or subcontractors can be time consuming and require immaculate preparation. Preparing all the presentations both domestically and internationally to a very high standard is a must. These preparations can be done at an international subcontractor's site or at your domestic site. Sometimes, these meetings can be at the customer's site. Who is going to present what? Who needs help for the preparations? International travel, pre-customer meetings, arrangements for the customer outside the meetings, etc., will take a large amount of time. As a rule of thumb, 90 percent of the work is in preparation and 10 percent in presentation for a customer's visit.

Especially, preparing international sites that are not used to your customer's expectations will be challenging and may require extensive up-front preparation at that particular site.

Something that is outside of your control can also happen at the customer's. The customer can remove your project manager and install a new one right in the heat of executing the project. In such a case, the new project manager from a Japanese customer wanted to visit all three international manufacturing and assembly sites as soon as possible. It took two weeks to prepare and visit all three sites with the new project manager. Time spent and costs for such unexpected changes at the customer's are unrecoverable but it has to be done. You have to do all you can to bring the customer's new project manager up to speed on the project, gain his confidence, and teach him the history of the project. This way he will be a good ally in seeing the project through to a successful completion.

Subcontractor Management

During project execution, subcontractor management is very critical to the project's success. Subcontractor management is effected with the help of vendor engineers, quality engineers, or purchasing agents who are mostly part-time members of the team. Controlling domestic and international subcontractors can be overwhelming. There can be many levels of subcontractor control, namely, from a simple weekly telephone call to get a task status, to implanting a full-time engineer at the subcontractor's facilities. Again, periodic face-to-face meetings with the critical subcontractor at his company's facilities are a must. Videoconferences or teleconferences always give you a rosy picture of how things are progressing at your subcontractor's site. You might be very surprised to see the actual progress of your task at your subcontractor's when you visit the latter's facilities. Some international subcontractors give a low bid and get the contract, but they cannot deliver on time and conform to all the specifications, standards, and certification requirements.

For example, it might be very appealing costwise to hand a subcontract to a casting house in China for a complicated piece of component. However, travel costs, inspection costs, misunderstandings in specifications and standards, reworks, and delivery delays will make that appealing cost balloon out of control very fast.

Face-to-face meetings with the subcontractor should go beyond a conference room. During the design, construction, and testing of the equipment, you should be able to enter a subcontractor's and his subsupplier's facilities for the purpose of inspecting documents, materials, workmanship, and testing related to the project. You should be able to show the subcontractor's facilities to your customers and regulatory agency inspectors with confidence and with a good feeling that they are a part of your overall project team. After all, they will not let you down and therefore drag the project down.

The following case study in subcontractor management shows the unexpected things that can happen during project execution.

In a one-year project to design, manufacture, test, and supply an automated system to a Norwegian customer, a California company chose a Dutch subcontractor for the hydraulic cylinders that were required for the system. The finished system was going to Malaysia for final installation and usage. This Dutch subcontractor had a good and quality delivery record from previous contracts.

The hydraulic cylinder subcontractor's special steel subsupplier, who was German, delayed the special steel delivery from their mill by four months. The raw material delay news came suddenly from the Dutch subcontractor after three months into the project that had a total project duration of six months.

The best improvement the Dutch subcontractor could do to the three-month raw material delay was a month. Therefore, it would push the delivery of hydraulic cylinders to California by three months, which in turn would delay the delivery of the assembled and tested systems to the customer from California by at least two months. All shipments of this heavy equipment were cost accounted and scheduled to be sea freighted. Liquidated damages for delayed shipment to the customer were more than the hydraulic cylinder subcontractor's purchase order amount. Also, at this juncture in the project, the hydraulic cylinder design was completed by the Dutch subcontractor and approved by the company and the required regulatory agency.

As the project manager, the first action was to call an upper management meeting in the next 24 hour to find a mutually agreeable and minimum-damage solution. The project manager had to prepare a preliminary options list and cost benefit analyses of all the options for the meeting.

Preliminary options:

1. The company had to take control of the situation. The program manager was given full responsibility to take charge of the situation.
2. Find another hydraulic cylinder supplier who had the special steel material in stock and cancel the contract with the Dutch subcontractor.
3. Find a steel distributor around the world who had the special steel material in stock and
3. a. Airfreight the special steel, weighing 30 t, to Holland for fabrication and assembly. Then airfreight the finished hydraulic cylinders, weighing 3 t each × 20 cylinders, to California for system assembly and test. Then airfreight the completed systems, weighing 15 t each × 10 systems, to the final destination in Malaysia, or
3. b. Airfreight the special steel to the company manufacturing facility in California for fabrication, assembly, and test of hydraulic cylinders. Then airfreight the ten completed systems to their final destination in Malaysia.
4. Visit the original German steel mill with the subcontractor and with the customer to negotiate an earlier delivery, i.e., reduce the delay time from four months to two months by offering overtime work and extra funding for the material.

After several hours of brainstorming the options with the upper management, the following solution was reached:

Option 1 in the preceding list was approved unanimously, and all the personnel that the program manager requested were assigned to him to remedy the situation.

Option 2 was dismissed because the hydraulic design was already completed and fully approved. It would be quite an undertaking to start the whole process from scratch and gain time and complete it within budget.

Option 3b would have cost more and the personnel allocated to build the hydraulic cylinders at the company facilities would have delayed the other assembly and test operations for the project.

Option 4 was dismissed after several discussions with the subcontractor. Apparently, the German mill got a large steel order and the Dutch subcontractor's small order was pushed out. Also, the vacation month of August in Europe affected the delay. Our subcontractor already discussed all options with the German subsupplier without any success.

Option 3a was the route that the company upper management, with the help of the project manager, decided to take. The company launched an all-out effort to locate the special steel around the world. In two days, it found the special steel with a distributor in the United States at a premium price as compared to the

German mill price, and the company helped the Dutch subcontractor financially to purchase and airfreight the raw material to Holland. The Dutch subcontractor, in return, gave top priority and devoted overtime work to complete the hydraulic cylinders on an agreed-upon schedule. However, the company had to airfreight all the hydraulic cylinders from Holland to California on its own nickel in order to be able to ship the completed systems to the customer with a month delay. The company and subcontractor negotiations were done face-to-face with the subcontractor's president in Holland.

After a viable solution was found, a new project schedule was created, and then the customer was informed about the situation by teleconferencing. From the time the special material delay was learned from the subcontractor to the time the customer was informed with a solution took five working days. All the work that went into finding a favorable solution through all the time zones was discussed in detail with the customer. The customer accepted a month's delay in the system delivery without applying any liquidated damages, considering all the efforts and financial sacrifices the company was making to remedy the situation. After all the hassle, the company did not have to airfreight the completed systems to Malaysia because the overall project was also delayed.

Helping the Dutch subcontractor to recover from this delay worked out to be a win–win situation financially for both parties. The subcontractor worked very hard to finish the project on an agreed modified schedule. If the company had decided to squeeze the subcontractor into the corner and knocked them out to get the job done, the whole project would have failed. Also, the company assigned a full-time resident engineer to monitor the subcontractor's progress continuously after this event.

This one delay on a critical component cost the company a black eye, and the company lost the customer's confidence in it for future work. Errors were made by the project manager in risk management and subcontractor management. Such a critical item should have been checked daily, and backup options should have been considered early on in the project. Also the subcontractor's contracts should have been drawn up with delivery dates tied to penalty clauses for on-time deliveries and for on-time receipt of critical materials from the subcontractor's subsuppliers. The company should have implanted a resident engineer to monitor progress, nonconformance issues, and on-location risk management decisions from the beginning of the project.

Lessons learned from this subcontractor management fiasco were

1. Obtain a detailed plan for sourcing critical items before giving a purchase order to a subcontractor. Also, make sure that the backup sources for the critical items are determined and written into the purchase-order contract. Add penalty clauses into the purchase-order contract for the critical items delivery dates to the subcontractor.
2. Consider the effects of vacation times and plant shutdown times to the sources of critical items and to subcontractor deliveries.

3. Consider the risks of being bumped by a large order for critical items. It would have been a less risky approach to go to a steel distributor instead of a steel mill from the beginning and share the 10 percent cost premium instead of trying to squeeze out all the cost breaks.
4. Monitor the critical subcontractor and its subsuppliers very closely.

Careful selection of domestic and international subcontractors, not weighing heavily the cost factor during the subcontract rewarding process, and a strong subcontractor management group on your project team will make the project progress smoothly.

Dealing with Upper Management

Informing the status of the project to upper management regularly and getting its advice to solve the project's major issues go a long way during project execution.

Monthly status meetings are recommended. These meetings should cover schedule-performance and cost-performance indices for every task group, good news about the project, major issues and their solutions, customer's overall project status, and upcoming milestones. If an upper manager cannot make it to the monthly status meeting, meet one-on-one with him or her. Similar monthly status meetings should be held with the upper managers of international project sites. Document-controlled meeting minutes also should be distributed to all the involved upper managers.

Another type of upper management meetings are emergency meetings related to the project. For timely risk management, these emergency meetings can be held at short notice if there is a quorum. You should always go to these emergency meetings with concise description of the issue at hand and proposed solutions. Document-controlled emergency meeting minutes also should be distributed to all the involved upper managers.

Always invite the involved upper managers to important customer meetings, your team's project celebrations, patent certificate award meetings, project ending meetings, etc.

Sometimes, an upper manager can interfere with your project and try to pull the design that your team members are working toward by what he or she thinks is the best approach. If such circumstances occur, talk to the interfering upper manager, listen to him or her, and propose a team meeting along with him or her to brainstorm the design. Ask the upper manager kindly to go through you if he or she wants a shift in design direction, and not go directly to your team members to confuse them and get them stressed out.

On some occasions upper managers, both domestic and international, will go to your team members, give them little tasks, ask them to do some favors, and thus distract them to cause delays in your project. They are the big bosses and you have to obey them, especially in the Pacific Rim countries. As an international project manager, if you hear such distractions, you should go to the upper managers who are abusing your project team and ask them kindly to stop it or go through you if they have a request from your team members. Of course, this situation is much more difficult to control in international project sites. You have to keep asking your project leader at the international project site if there are any distractions to your team members, and handle these situations without any delay.

Regulatory Agency Management

If your project is to design a motor vehicle or components that go into a motor vehicle in the United States, you will be dealing with the federal motor vehicle safety standards and regulations. If your project is to design a system for an offshore oil platform in the Gulf of Mexico, you will be dealing with American Bureau of Shipping (ABS) design standards and regulations and Underwriters Laboratories testing certifications. If your offshore oil platform project is for a European country, you will be dealing with Det Norske Veritas (DNV) design standards and regulations and CENELEC (European Committee for Electrotechnical Standardization) testing certifications.

In the country your project system is going to end up in, the hazardous area classifications, temperature classifications, explosion protection classifications, ingress protection classifications, etc., can be quite different. You have to know all the regulatory agencies' classification and certification requirements for the project by heart. You have to determine which of your subcontractors have to deal with which regulatory agency for design and testing.

For example, in some cases, your subcontractors might not want to deal with a regulatory agency's design and test-certification process. Some subcontractors might not have the expertise or the personnel to go through it. You might have to help them tackle the hurdles with regulatory agencies.

You have to know your contacts and their backups at the regulatory agencies. You have to be very responsive to the agencies' requests and inquiries so that their progress in certification is not bogged down because of you. The design packages that are submitted to the regulatory agencies should conform to their request to the letter. All documents submitted to the regulatory agencies should be first released in your document control system. A typical offshore oil platform system design package for ABS submission contains all the design drawings, all the design calculations with summaries, all components specifications and test certificates for hazardous areas, all material specifications and test certificates, and all hydraulic and electrical schematics showing each component's design safety rating and hazardous area classification.

Depending upon the complexity of your project, these regulatory agency submittals can be over ten volumes and thousands of pages. You have to plan appropriately for these submittals. You have to get them checked thoroughly so that simple omissions or errors do not delay the design certification process. After a design package is submitted, follow up with your contact at the regulatory agency periodically. Help him or her to go through the difficult-to-understand sections of the design package.

Similar detailed planning goes for component certification testing. Certified test houses and regulatory agency representatives have to be planned and scheduled appropriately so that the tests can go without a glitch. It is highly recommended that similar pre-certification tests be performed before the regulatory agencies arrive.

In one of the projects for a European Union country, the control console designer used a component that was only certified by the Underwriters Laboratories in the United States for hazardous area application and not by CENELEC for European Union applications. DNV noticed this during the design review process and rejected the component. The regulatory agency's design review occurred after the consoles were built because the design package was not submitted to it in a timely fashion. The project manager took the risk of building the consoles without certification and expected no glitches in the certification process. The control console certification was delayed until a CENELEC-certified replacement component was found and design drawings were revised and resubmitted to the regulatory agency. The old component was replaced in all the consoles, and they were all retested. This one simple oversight delayed a milestone shipment by two months and cost the project a bundle.

Design and test certificates for the project should be controlled documents, and they should be formally submitted to your customers.

During the execution of a project, in addition to managing the domestic and international project teams, customers, subcontractors, upper management, and regulatory agencies, the international engineering project manager also has to focus on several other important factors. These factors that affect project execution can be categorized as surprises, errors, listening, practical solutions, whatever it takes, meetings, status reports, confidentiality and intellectual property, risk management, fire fighting, adapting to change, controlling the project, training, and timeoff.

Surprises

In an international project execution, as the project manager, you have to deal with many issues that cannot be forecasted or known from the beginning of the project. There are a lot of surprises that make the project execution a great challenge.

An example of such a project execution occurred in Malaysia. The object of this international project was to set up a magnetic recording head assembly factory in Malaysia in six months from scratch, that is, ramp up production from zero to 200,000 assemblies per week. This meant twenty just-in-time semiautomated production lines inside and outside a clean room operating in three shifts, 24 × 7.

The engineering project manager chose six senior engineers for the team, namely, two process engineers, two quality engineers, and two test engineers. A project plan was prepared for the general manager of the Malaysian factory who was a Malay, not an American. From cultural and networking points of view, it is always advisable to have a native general manager.

The project plan called for hiring and training of 20 process engineers, 120 supervisors, and 1200 operators and inspectors, all Malaysian, in six months. Hiring tests were prepared together with the human resources group. Especially good eyesight and good dexterity were needed for the operators and inspectors. Everyone had to be trained in statistical process control procedures for high-volume production, in clean-room procedures, in electrostatic discharge protection procedures, etc. All the process and test engineers had to be trained in equipment and tooling calibration and maintenance.

The training was done in pyramid ordering. The U.S.-based process engineers trained the Malaysian counterparts in tooling, calibration, process instructions, statistical process controls, and document control procedures. The Malaysian process engineers in turn trained the line supervisors, who in turn trained the operators. Similar training process was applied to test personnel and inspectors. All critical process instructions were translated into Bahasa Malay, and processes were videotaped and sound effects were done in the language for ease of training and to avoid any misinterpretation.

For tooling, an in-house tool repair shop was put together. For precision machining, outside subcontractors were qualified. During all the ongoing tasks, the project manager realized the deficiencies that he had not thought about in the project planning and had to correct these dynamically as the project progressed.

One of the surprise behaviors was the prompt meeting attendance. All the attendees wandered into the meeting conference room five to ten minutes late. It was a latitude and attitude issue. The project manager asked the general manager to resolve this issue. They sat down together and devised a plan as to how to correct this lackadaisical behavior. The general manager circulated a stern memorandum to everyone to be on time for all meetings; otherwise, disciplinary action would be taken against late-arriving individuals. Everyone started to show up on time.

Another surprise behavior came from the general manager himself for the new factory. He never left his office and walked the assembly lines to motivate his people or to listen to their complaints. The project manager asked the general manager to be more interactive and visit the production lines at least twice a day, one for the day shift and one for the swing shift. The latter listened to project manager's advice, and also came in early twice a week to visit the night-shift lines.

Another important issue for the Malay engineers was the lack of knowledge in magnetic recording. The project manager set up classes to train them in the elementary theories and concepts of magnetic recording and the effects of manufacturing parameters on magnetic recording.

Another surprise was operating in a wet and high-humidity environment with unreliable utilities in Malaysia. The clean-room humidity controls had to be beefed up and tied into a backup power circuit. Each test equipment had to have an uninterruptible power supply with a voltage regulator.

Contamination control was also another challenging issue. None of the Malaysians were used to the procedures and disciplines of a class 10 clean-room environment. They were all trained and constantly audited for clean-room procedures. Compressed air lines, air ionizers, clean-room filters, operator's gloves, etc., were upgraded to eliminate contamination.

The U.S. team members had to be sent home periodically so that they could satisfy their personal needs at the home front. They were also awarded extended side trips for rest and recreation. A couple of U.S. engineers brought their families and lived with them in Malaysia for the duration of their duties. The company provided them with furnished houses and paid for their families' trip.

The U.S. team members had to learn Malaysian culture. They attended Malaysian weddings, dinners, parties, and other company events. Malaysia is blessed with a multiculture society, namely Malays, Chinese, and Indians. The plant had a special praying room for the Malaysian Muslims. They took special breaks during the day for their praying. U.S. engineers were invited to the Hindu religious festival of Thaipusam to observe the spectacular pilgrimage and practices.

In a dynamic and fast-paced project such as this one, everything had to run like a well-oiled machine. Project status was given daily to U.S. headquarters by teleconferencing and to the Malaysian general manager during a daily face-to-face meeting. Any issue that came up had to be resolved very quickly with the support of upper management. Daily meetings were held with the U.S. and Malaysian engineers as a team. All the action items and their owners and due dates were listed.

These meetings were expanded down the pecking order to supervisors, operators, and inspectors at the beginning of every shift. All the tooling issues, information from previous shifts, and out-of-control control charts were all discussed and solutions put in place for every production line in every shift.

Another surprise that came to surface was the need for extra spare parts for the automated assembly equipment. It was very difficult to obtain simple things like microscope bulbs in a timely fashion. An extended spare-parts list was generated, purchased in the United States, and stocked in Malaysia to avoid any line downtime.

Customer factory qualifications were a part of the project. Without customer qualification, volume production could not have started. Customer visits were arranged to the utmost detail. Everyone at the factory was made aware of the customer's expectations. All documentation from operator qualification records to control chart out-of-control point corrective action reports were pre-audited. Everyone was ready and hyped up for the customer's visit. Customer's production line qualification went without a glitch. The customer qualified the production lines, and volume production shipments started within six months.

In another example, during the execution of a data communication module design, an upper manager from the headquarters came to the design center and announced in an all-hands meeting, to everyone's surprise, that he was closing the design center down. For the project manager, things went all of a sudden topsy-turvy. The project team's morale went to the pits, but he had to complete the project deliverables under these unstable conditions. In these extreme cases, the project manager's very close association with team members to complete the project is very crucial.

During project execution, surprising events, inquiries, and requests can come from any segment of the project structure. These situations can range from equipment interface layouts, overlooked specifications, nonconforming specifications, delays in deliveries, canceled projects, etc., to unavailable raw materials. Prompt and timely response to the customer's surprising events, inquiries and requests, to that of the subcontractor, to that of the regulatory agency's, to that of the upper management's are very crucial. Prompt, timely, and complete response to a surprising event, inquiry, or request gives impetus to a project and keeps the project rolling under the guidance of a successful project manager.

If your customer is in Europe and you are in California, you have a time advantage in responding to your customer's surprising events, inquiries, and requests. By the time you get into your office at 8 a.m., all such from your European customer accumulate in your e-mail inbox. You can read them and prioritize them, search for answers for, and respond to every one of them before your day is over. Your customer will be delighted to see your prompt answers when they come into their office in the morning. Even if you cannot complete the answer to a surprising event, an inquiry, or a request in a day, send an acknowledgment message saying that you need another day to research and would be able to respond to them properly. Silence and delays in response to surprises are the worst enemies of a project manager.

Errors

Errors will occur during the execution of a project. They can come from a designer's calculation, a subcontractor's machining of a hole pattern, or a customer's mistyped specification. We are all human, and errors will occur.

When a team member makes an error during the execution of a project, do not reprimand him or her immediately. For example, a design error was made during a vehicle motor mount stress analysis, namely, the moment of inertia for a motor mount beam was miscalculated. The design error surfaced after the first two prototype vehicles were built. The designer came to the project manager with a red face and announced the error. It was an honest mistake. The project manager asked the designer to correct the calculations and get them checked by another engineer. The project manager gathered all the designers for a lessons-learned meeting, explained the situation, and brainstormed the solutions so that such an error does not occur again. The solution was to implement a dual and independent checking system for the critical calculations. The two vehicles were retrofitted with the new motor mounts, and after that incidence, no design errors occurred during the execution of the project.

In another example, a designer put the wrong voltage control panel light part numbers on the drawing bill of materials. The drawing checker also missed the error and it was overlooked during the design review meeting. The solution to this error was to make it a requirement to put a detailed part's description on a drawing in addition to the supplier's part number when the bill of materials was generated.

Upper management can make errors, too. In a complicated hydraulic manifold design subproject, the project manager asked upper management to fund a 3-D CAD (computer-aided design) software and training for the complicated hydraulic manifold design and to upgrade the company's design tools for future projects. Upper management decided to go with the already available 2-D CAD system to design the hydraulic manifold. It's logic behind the decision was that the company had made many hydraulic manifold designs successfully in the past using the 2-D CAD system. Why should the company invest in a 3-D CAD design tool at this time for this complicated manifold? The design engineer did his best to calculate all the tolerance stack-ups and place the inlet and outlet ports on the manifold design. During the beta test stage of the manifold, circuit logic tests showed that there was a break between one of the pressure passages and a return passage. Machining tolerances and not enough spacing between the passages caused this error. Manifold had to be redesigned, rebuilt, and re-beta-tested. This delayed the project for a month. One tolerance stack-up error and one minimum-spacing violation error were missed by the designer and checker during the design review process among hundreds of dimensions. It cost the project and the company much more than the cost of a 3-D CAD tool. The upper management learned its lesson the hard way and authorized engineering to get the 3-D CAD software for future projects.

In another example, a subcontractor did not calibrate the load cells to the whole range of the specification that was on the drawings. The load cells came into the plant and were accepted by receiving inspection and released to production. The error was discovered during the assembly process. All the load cells had to be shipped back to the subcontractor. The subcontractor was embarrassed. He blamed the error on a new and an inexperienced test engineer. He did all he could to expedite the extended calibrations and ship the load cells back in a week. He also presented the company with a corrective actions list that was implemented to prevent further errors. The company's vendor engineer visited the load-cell subcontractor, verified the implementation of the corrective actions, and recommended that the supplier not be blacklisted. Similar corrective actions were taken at the company's receiving inspection to prevent any hiccups in the future.

Sometimes your subcontractor can be the sole source. You cannot blacklist him or her. You have to work with the person to improve his or her operations so that they can be error free.

The customer's project team also makes mistakes. For example, an international customer's inspector forgot to include spare parts into his final inspection, acceptance, and release for shipment reports. The equipment was shipped to Korea along with its spare parts, but the customer had a lot of difficulty getting the spare parts out of customs because the shipment items list and the final inspection, acceptance, and release for shipment list did not match item by item. The inspector had to revise his reports and present them again to the Korean customs for formal release of the spare parts, and present them again to the customer's finance department for the payment process to begin. Any simple discrepancies between the shipped-items list and the final inspection, acceptance, and release-for-shipment list can cause a lot of delays at customs and with payment releases. The solution was to implement a dual-checking system for the customer's final inspection, acceptance, and release-for-shipment report between the company's quality control and shipping departments before the customer's inspector left the company facilities.

If the errors keep occurring and the designer or the subcontractor does not listen to the suggested corrective actions, then the project manager has to take more extraordinary actions such as removing the team member from the project team or disqualifying the subcontractor, if possible.

Listening

Listening to others and weighing in their inputs before making a decision is a very powerful virtue in life and especially in international program management. During the execution of a project, you have to be a good listener. You have to listen to domestic and international team members, customers, subcontractors, and upper management.

You have to listen to the inputs even when they are coming from a person outside the project team. For example, range tests for a newly designed electric vehicle were to be performed simulating the stop-and-go environment and loads during its usage. It was difficult to find an appropriate road or track to perform the range tests. One of the secretaries suggested that, perhaps the close-by airport runway might be the solution, the airport closed to air traffic after midnight to 6 a.m., and they might allow the usage of their runway for the range tests. The issue was discussed with the airport authorities, and they allowed the range tests to be performed on their runway after midnight for five days. Also, sand bags were used to simulate passenger loads. A secretary's great suggestion saved the day for the project and gained at least a week of time in schedule performance. The project manager did not forget to get two tickets for the secretary and her spouse to see her favorite basketball team.

Another example of listening is in dimensioning the drawing of a complicated machined component. It will be good to show that drawing before formal release to the machinist who is going to manufacture it and get his inputs. He or she might not have the right tools to measure the dimensions from the datums that are called out in the drawing. It would be good to listen to the mechanist and modify the drawing so that it can be manufactured with ease and without any misunderstandings and mistakes.

Similar listening advice goes for manufacturing instructions for volume-production line operators. You should take the draft of the manufacturing instructions to the most experienced operator on your production line and get his or her inputs and enhance the manufacturing instructions accordingly. Such dialogues reduce defects and make your product superior.

Another example for listening comes from your subcontractors. If you are designing a complicated component that will be produced by casting, show it to your casting subcontractor and get his inputs on tolerances, stress relieving procedures, nondestructive examination procedures, acceptance criteria regarding indications and weld repairs, material alloy callouts, cost-reduction suggestions, etc., before releasing the drawing. Your casting supplier has a lot of experience in his field. Listen to him or her and make your project execution easier by being proactive rather than reactive.

Another good example cited here came from listening to the chief financial officer of a computer component manufacturing company. The project manager was presenting the monthly project status indices to the upper management. Cost performance indices degraded after the annual salary increases went into effect. During the bidding process for the multi-year and fixed-price contract, the salespeople did not take into account the annual salary increases. The chief financial officer suggested that cost performance indices should be calculated by showing the salary increases and also by not taking them into account. This was also a fair way of assessing the project's cost performance. The project manager thanked the chief financial officer for her suggestion and started to evaluate the project's cost performance with and without salary increases.

Listening to others can bring advantages not only to the project but also to the whole company. In such a case, a magnetic head manufacturing engineer came up with a novel suspension design during a disk drive head stack assembly project. The new design was a low profile one and it was much cheaper to manufacture. The project manager encouraged the manufacturing engineer to file for a patent. During a patent application review session, the intellectual property (IP) attorney for the company suggested that the low-profile suspension design should be expanded to all possible assembly configurations at the support end to make it more generic. The project manager and the manufacturing engineer thanked the IP attorney for his great suggestion and worked together for a week to enhance the new suspension design for other possible stack assemblies. A broadly applicable patent was granted, and the company benefited handsomely from listening to the IP attorney.

Practical Solutions

During the execution of an international project, there are many tasks for which the project manager can never see light at the end of the tunnel. It feels like all the moons have to align so that the task mountain can be conquered. As the project manager, you have to promote practical solutions to difficult issues that come up during the execution of a project. Practical solutions can relieve pressure from the team members and save money and time for the project.

For example, during the ground-up design of a rotary engine, cooling fluid flow simulation through engine water passages were planned by using finite element methods (FEM). The FEM process was timely and costly, needed fast and large computer-processing capacity, and did not simulate the cavitating regions well. The project team brainstormed the situation and decided to build engine body models from plexiglass and simulate water-flow behavior in the engine water passages at a university fluids laboratory. This type of visual simulation gave faster results, and the cavitating regions were eliminated by iterating the design with confidence.

Another example of being practical is in communication. A German bus body builder's engineers and project manager for an electric bus project did not have good grasp of English. They made obvious mistakes in understanding the fine points of the specifications and in daily communications. For example, the electric bus ground clearance during travel was going to be high, and the bus level was going to be lowered to its minimum ground clearance height during passenger loading and unloading using air suspensions. The German project manager and the design engineers did not fully understand the design concept and the detailed specifications. Communicating in English was generating errors and delays in the project and was a burden on the German subcontractor. Immediately, a German translator with automotive terminology background was found. All the relevant specifications were translated into German. Also, all the daily communications from Germany came in German and were translated into English, and the responses were also in German. This type of setup made life much easier for the German bus body builder. Also errors were avoided by elimination of the language barrier. The cost of translation was a small token compared to an error-free subassembly.

Another good example of being practical is in the design of experiments for wafer process optimization. In a new wafer fabrication process optimization project, the project team came up with a two-level full factorial design of experiments with six main effects. This meant 64 experiments. Each experimental wafer lot took three wafers due to defects and scraps. Also, there had to be 64 follow-on confirmation experiments. The project manager asked the project team to be more practical, and asked them to evaluate all the main effect interactions and to come up with a simpler fractional factorial design for the experiments. The team came back in a week with a 16-experiment fractional factorial design. The reduced number of wafer lots saved both cost and time for the project. On top of everything, the management of 64 different experiments in a wafer fabrication environment is a nightmare. There are a lot of errors made in different shifts, and the results become suspicious. Optimized wafer fabrication process started two weeks earlier than scheduled thanks to a simpler and a condensed fractional factorial design of experiments.

Good examples of practical solutions are encountered in mechanical designs of components and assemblies. Most mechanical design engineers tend to use tight tolerances to avoid headaches during assembly. Tight tolerancing increases machining and inspection costs and skyrockets reworks. A good example of this is to use a loosely toleranced slotted hole pattern design instead of a tightly toleranced round hole pattern design for assemblies. A productive design review process during the project execution phase that involves the machinists who will build the components, and the assemblers who will assemble the components, will generate many practical solutions that will simplify the design, bring the cost down, and save time for the project.

Whatever It Takes

During the execution of a project, the project manager has to do whatever it takes to complete a task without damaging his integrity and breaking the laws. As the driver of the project, the project manager has to promote creative solutions for stalled tasks, for antiquated company procedures, and for international deadlocks. A winning project team always has a determined quarterback who comes up with unusual plays and does whatever it takes to win the game.

A good example of determination to complete a task was experienced in a passenger-car body design in Europe. When the car body was being designed, NASA Structural Analysis (NASTRAN) was the only FEM design tool around. This tool was too expensive, and there was not enough computer memory to run the model at the design center or in the city that the design center was located. Time to market was of essence, and the car body specification had a low-weight target. The stress analysis engineer wrote the finite element model program, modeled the car body, and traveled four hundred miles to another city to run the calculations at nights at the computer of another organization. The results were brought back to the design center. The prototype body was built and design iterations were done by repeating the calculations and going back and forth to the city where the large-memory computer resided. The team did whatever it took to finish the car body design in one year. This example occurred in the 1970s when powerful workstations and Internet communications were a dream. However, the concept still applies today. Some tasks might require new tools and imaginative sacrifices for completion on time and within budget.

Another example is in helping a department that is short-handed due to illness. The quality department in a major offshore equipment design project had to complete the inspection and test requirement documents as a milestone for the customer. The quality department was very shorthanded and overworked. The project manager formed a mini-team outside the quality department and got all the documents prepared on time. The quality department only reviewed and made comments on these documents and approved them for document control. Such interdepartmental support helps relieve the pressure and get things done on time, and are common in smaller companies.

You might also have to push to improve company procedures during the execution of a project. In one such case, a company did not have an efficient emergency material review board process. The existing process was not dynamic and fast enough to respond to nonconformances. The project manager held a meeting with the upper management of the company and proposed a much more responsive daily material review board system and an emergency material review board system. Both systems were approved by the upper management and got implemented after minor modifications. This companywide improvement saved the project precious time in responding to nonconformances, especially by the subcontractors, and gained the company a very responsive material review board system.

If the project manager is determined, international deadlocks can also be resolved. For example, during a system design, manufacturing, and installation project for an African country, a New Zealand subcontractor was chosen for a special programmable logic controller. When the time came to install the system and train the local team, the project manager asked the New Zealand subcontractor to send an engineer to the African country for three weeks to perform these tasks. The New Zealand subcontractor came back with a surprising answer. During that time the New Zealand government put travel restrictions on this particular African nation and no one with a New Zealand passport could travel there. The panic button was on. The project manager discussed all the possible options with the subcontractor. He asked the subcontractor if they had qualified engineers who worked for its distributors in other countries that do not have travel restrictions to the African country in question. The subcontractor searched for other qualified candidates in their distribution system. It found a qualified South African engineer who worked for its South African distributor and who could perform the tasks in a timely manner. The driver, namely, the project manager, did whatever it took and found a plausible solution to keep the project chugging along.

Meetings

Meetings are the backbone of a project. They hold the whole project together. Meetings can break a project, or make a project very successful if used efficiently and decisively.

Project kickoffs, design reviews, risk management, buy-ins, project status presentations, team communications, customer milestones, subcontractor milestones, etc., all require domestic, international, or virtual meetings. These can be team meetings, subgroup meetings, individual team member meetings, fun and morale-boosting team get-togethers, customer meetings, subcontractor meetings, and upper management meetings. Meeting preparation, meeting management, meeting minutes format, and meeting minutes document control and distribution should all be standardized at the planning phase of a project.

Sometimes you might have to dodge the standard meeting methods. For example, if you want to call an emergency meeting, you might have to go to every member's office and invite him or her to a verbal agenda meeting, instead of going to a formal, say, MS Outlook, meeting organizer. On the other hand, periodic meetings, customer meetings, subcontractor meetings, and upper management meetings should be properly prepared, and the people involved informed well ahead of time, and executed according to a pre-published meeting agenda. If in a meeting a subject is allocated a certain duration, and if the meeting runs over that duration, reschedule another meeting to finish that particular subject. Meetings cost projects a lot of time and therefore money. Inefficiencies in meetings are a given fact. These meeting inefficiencies can affect the schedule and cost of the project tremendously. Therefore, meeting control and sticking to an agenda are required. Especially in upper management meetings, upper managers tend to deviate from the subject under discussion and digress to other projects and effects of the present situation on other projects, etc. Gently but firmly bring them back on track.

Meeting minutes should be a controlled document. Action items lists with the owners, required action completion dates, and actual action completion dates should be distributed to everyone involved. Sometimes action items are given to a person who is not attending the meeting. In such a case the project manager should go to that person, explain the action item, and what is expected from him or her. The project manager should also emphasize the action item completion date.

Before a design review meeting with the customer, always do a dry run. Make sure that the customer approves the meeting agenda prior to the meeting and add the items they would like to discuss during the meeting. Prepare a separate room for the customer to discuss issues in privacy among themselves. Make communication tools available to them, such as Internet connections, telephones, faxes, printers, etc.

Make sure you have extra bulbs for the slide projector, overhead projector, or the laptop computer external projection system. Know how to use all the presentation tools. Try them before the meeting and make sure that everything is operational. Sometimes even simple things like blackboard cleaners, proper felt pens, notepads, pens, pencils, and erasers are overlooked and cause disruptions during a meeting.

Also, catering is crucial to an important and long meeting. Coffee, tea, cookies, lunches, sometimes dinners, and breaks are important ingredients of a successful meeting.

Scribing the meeting minutes has to be assigned to someone who will be present during the whole meeting. The meeting minutes scriber should be announced at the beginning of the meeting. Also, the official meeting minutes distribution process should be announced at the beginning of the meeting. Sometimes the meeting minutes have to be first read, edited, and approved by the customer before its official release in document control and distribution. If time is of essence for the action items, a preliminary version of the meeting minutes should be distributed to action items owners in order not to lose precious time during customer approval and document control release processes.

When you are announcing a meeting, if you state the meeting time as 4/6/06 8–10 a.m., this might mean quiet different times to different people in different countries. Is the meeting on 6 April 2006 or on 4 June 2006? Does it start at 8 a.m. Pacific Standard Time?

A very clear meeting time callout will eliminate any errors and frustrations worldwide. For example, if you are scheduling a meeting with a South Korean subcontractor, you might say the teleconferencing will start on 26 April 2006, Wednesday, 4 p.m. Pacific Standard Time (PST) (27 April 2006, Thursday, 10 a.m. South Korean time) and will last for two hours. You will initiate the meeting by calling Mr. H. I. Kim on his telephone number 011-82-622-233-5478.

Meeting protocols are very important in international project management. If you are attending a customer design review meeting in Japan, the project team who travels to Japan sits on the side of the conference table away from the conference room entry door in a ranking order commensurate with experience and responsibility. The Japanese customer team walks in with ten people against your three. Handshakes, introductions, and card exchanges are very formal. It would be very helpful to your customer if you and your team members have dual-language business cards with pictures on them. Depending upon how well you know the person and his rank, the introductory exchanges vary considerably. Names and their pronunciations are very important. If you can learn the names and their pronunciations, and the ranks of the customer's participants ahead of the meeting, that would be very helpful.

Opening welcoming remarks are made by the senior ranking members of both parties. When the meeting is at customer's facility, let the customer side lead the meeting. Give them your proposed agenda items and let them arrange the order. Then, as you start going over the agenda items one by one, the room starts to fill with cigarette smoke from at least ten sources. You are bombarded with detailed questions about all facets of the project. You make a statement and it is translated into Japanese. Then they make a statement and it is translated into English. It is good to have a bilingual engineer on your team during these meetings so that you do not miss any fine points lost in translation or during the exchanges that they have among themselves. You have to watch like a hawk that nothing is lost or diverted during these exchanges. In most countries in the Far East, they hear you and acknowledge it with a head shake or with a "Hai, Domo" in Japan, but you have to make sure that they understand the point.

It is common to have design review meetings that last ten to twelve hours both domestically and internationally. Prepare yourself for the long ride. Get rid of your jet lag and be sharp during these long meetings. If you think that you are losing a debate and you feel that you have to regroup, call a timeout from the meeting and request to go to a private room to regroup or discuss a crucial point among your team members privately. In the final phase of the meeting, write down all the action items both by the customer and by your team with due dates and with owners. Get the customer to approve the meeting minutes and the action items before you leave.

Sometimes, due to time constraints and long hours, the meeting minutes and action items are proposed to be finalized later. Try to avoid this because there will be delays in completing the final version of the meeting minutes, and there can be some errors and misunderstandings in the delayed meeting minutes. This might cause delays in tasks and also cause misunderstanding as to what was agreed on at the meeting. Complete the meeting minutes and action items when everyone is there and everything is fresh in your minds. Being precise, accurate, and detailed in these meetings go a long way.

Teams complete the design review meeting and exchange bows and "Sayonaras". Your team is very tired, but the day is not finished yet. After these long meetings, you might have to go out to dinner and drinks in most countries. Your behavior at dinners and drinking events also shows your respect toward the culture and traditions of the country that you are in and builds your interpersonal relationship with your customer and your international team members. You have to be very polite if you do not want to follow their customs or traditions. For example, if you do not want to eat with your bare right hand or with a chopstick, politely ask for a fork. If you are the guest of honor and are offered to eat a monkey brain in Singapore or a jumping live fish in Japan, you can politely refuse and pass on to another dish. If everyone around the table is drinking from the same shot glass in South Korea to show their unity and friendship, you can politely refuse and decide not to drink that evening.

The final factory acceptance tests meeting with the customer and regulatory agency is always a special event. You are so close to the finish line, so do not blow it by cutting corners. Perform a complete pre-test with all the equipment, test fixtures, and data collection equipment. Make sure that everything is working properly before you invite the customer and the regulatory agency inspectors. All the test parameters and test documentation should be ready and released in document control and, if necessary, approved by the customer. Make sure that all the designers are present during the acceptance tests. Do not try to perform the final acceptance tests with only the test technicians. There might be questions and issues raised by the customer and by the inspectors that will require the designers' input. Avoid doing acceptance tests during weekends and holidays. You might not be able to reach some personnel who might be needed during the test, i.e., calibration technicians, stockroom personnel for spare parts, machinists, etc.

The punch list is a system discrepancy list compiled during the final factory acceptance tests. This list contains items such as improper nameplates, missing paint touchups, nonlubricated fasteners, etc., usually minor items that have to be completed before the final acceptance of the system by the customer and by the regulatory agency inspectors. All the items that the customer and the regulatory agency inspectors generate should be within the scope of the contract.

As an international engineering project manager, always carry a unit conversion chart from SI units to English units with you. It is very handy to be able to convert Joules to ft-lbf, MPa to psi, or mm to mil and vice versa simultaneously so that there is no communication gap between an SI-units-trained customer or inspector and an English-units-trained manufacturing engineer during a meeting.

If there is a major issue that comes up during the final factory acceptance tests, stop the test and call a meeting with the involved team members, the customer, and the inspectors. If the fix is long and involved, send the customer and the inspectors home. Do not let them stick around while the repairs or changes are done. You have to balance all these punch-list item tasks with shipment pressures from the upper management. Shipment means another milestone payment; that is what the upper management wants. However, as a project manager, you want to ship out a quality product for a satisfied customer. Most upper managers unfortunately think only of cash flow. Product quality and customer satisfaction are secondary priorities. Final factory acceptance testing and product shipment are the most exciting and hectic segments of a project, but a successful completion of these segments is very gratifying to the whole project team. Like a marathon runner, your team has finally clipped the finish line with success.

Final product acceptance tests are sometimes done in another country. For example, in a research safety vehicle design project for the U.S. Department of Transportation, the final vehicle acceptance testing was done in Germany. The completed research safety vehicle, test engineers, and test technicians were sent to Germany. The crash tests were performed there. The results of the crash tests were presented in a vehicle safety technical conference in Germany to the world community of vehicle safety design engineers. For such acceptance tests away from your factory, you have to be prepared very diligently with an extended list of spare parts and tools. Also, you have to send a diversified and an expert team to support the acceptance tests in a foreign country. The test team included vehicle designers, manufacturing engineers and technicians, and test engineers and technicians.

It is recommended that project status team meetings, domestic and international, are held at least once a month and at most every two weeks in a year-long project. The project manager should give the status of the overall project, including issues with the customers, subcontractors, regulatory agencies, etc. Task owners should summarize the status of their tasks while presenting solutions to the problematic segments.

Major scope changes should also be discussed in these project status team meetings. Minor scope changes that affect a task or a couple of tasks can be directly communicated to the task owners outside the team meeting. The design basis should be revised appropriately to reflect the scope changes in the project.

For upcoming important events such as a customer design review meeting or a final acceptance test meeting, a pre-meeting should be held. All the details of the upcoming important event should be discussed. Every team member's responsibility should be clearly defined. Even who is going to take the customer to lunch and dinner on a certain date should be identified ahead of time to avoid scheduling conflicts.

Periodic set-time teleconferences and videoconferences with international project sites, customers, and subcontractors should be agreed upon during the planning phase of the project or during the project kickoff meetings. Planning these conferences through many time zones and within small workable time slots might be challenging for an international engineering project manager.

For example, a customer for a data communication chip design was in Germany. Our design center was in California. The project manager used to have daily teleconferences with the customer at 8 a.m. PST (5 p.m. in Germany). These teleconferences lasted one to two hours, and a lot of chip design specification clarification issues were discussed and agreed upon during that time. The best way to make sure that nothing discussed or agreed was falling through the cracks was to record these teleconference sessions. Customer's permission was asked to record these teleconference sessions. After the teleconference, meeting notes were compared with the taped version and to make sure that nothing was missing. After completing the teleconferencing minutes, they were submitted to the customer for approval, and after the customer's approval, the meeting minutes became permanent records in the document control system. The completeness of these records helped the team to proceed with the chip design without missing any specification clarifications. The customer was also very pleased with accurate and very clear chip specifications.

In some projects you might have more than one customer. In other words, you have more than one boss to keep happy. For example, in an electric bus project funded by the U.S. Department of Transportation, the main customer was the Colorado Regional Transportation District. You had to keep both customer's project managers, namely, the U.S. Department of Transportation project manager and the Colorado Regional Transportation District project manager, informed of all issues, schedules, qualifications, tests, and meetings.

As an international project manager, you cannot be at two places at the same time and be able to attend all the project meetings. Tasks cannot wait for you. You have to make sure that all the other team members and project leaders who are on the project team follow the same meeting ground rules.

Status Reports

Another important task for a project manager is the periodic project status reports for the customer. Weekly, biweekly, or monthly written status reports for the customer should be standardized, should be in a format preferred by the customer, and document controlled. As a minimum cover, the following items should be included in a status report: project issues and their solutions listed chronologically, updated project schedule, contract scope changes, action items owed to the customer, action items owed by the customer, major subcontractors' issues, documents submitted to the customer, document comments received from the customer, and regulatory agency design and test certification status.

Preparing periodic status reports will need inputs from your international project sites, critical subcontractors, and other departments. Gathering all the inputs will take time and effort. If a project status report is to be delivered at the end of the month, it is advisable to start gathering all the pertinent information at least a week ahead of time. If the information gathered changes before the report goes out to the customer, you can always update the draft version before you release the customer's version, namely, revision one, into your document control on the last day of the month.

When you list in your status report all the action items that your customer owes you, emphasize the delinquent ones with the delinquency durations. In many instances the project manager has to push the customer to get things done. If you are dealing with a very busy or an unorganized customer's project manager, you have to manage the situation gently without antagonizing him or her. You might have to send documents over again if they are lost or misplaced by the customer. If you see an error, call the project manager and walk him through the error and its corrections. You might have to remind the project manager of some communication that occurred in the past and provide copies of the communication he or she might have misplaced. If the customer changes its project manager in the middle of the project, you have to bring the new project manager up to date regarding the project. Your detailed help to him or her will go a long way in speeding up the project.

If the customer starts to disagree on an issue that was settled in the past with the original project manager, your communication records will ease the tension and bring the disagreement to a fast closure. So, keeping project communication records in chronological order and in subject-related folders are crucial. Make sure that the electronic files are backed up at least daily by your information technology department. If the electronic filing system is not reliable, you have to revert, unfortunately, to a paper filing system.

Dealing with subcontractors is a mirror image of dealing with the customer, but this time you have to receive periodic status reports from the subcontractors because the project's success depends heavily on the critical subcontractors. You have to put the periodic status report requirements and the performance indices that you want to see into the subcontractor purchase order agreement. You might have to control some subcontractors much more tightly than the members of your domestic and international project team. Tight control means more frequent and detailed communication and presence at that subcontractor's. You have to help your subcontractor tackle issues and go over hurdles. You have to treat the subcontractor as an integral part of your project team.

For example, a Japanese magnetic recording head supplier was having low-yield issues and could not ramp up to expected production rates in a timely fashion.

Their weekly project status reports showed that the production yields were not improving, and the action items taken by the subcontractor to improve the yields were not satisfactory. The project manager made a firm and timely decision, got the upper management's approval, and sent a two-man team of senior manufacturing engineers to Japan for three months to help and improve the manufacturing yields of the magnetic recording head subcontractor for the project. This action proved to be successful and timely for a large customer's disk-drive production ramp.

Weekly or bimonthly project status reports arriving from a subcontractor might not tell the full story of how the project is going on. Periodic visits to the subcontractor are a must. A good subcontractor might not have a good design department but an excellent manufacturing group. Then help that subcontractor with the design and getting the design approved by regulatory agencies. A good subcontractor might be having difficulty in getting materials certified or welders qualified. Help your subcontractor to overcome these issues in a timely fashion. The project manager in charge of your project at the subcontractor's might quit in the middle of the project. You have to bring the new manager up to date. This interaction should be done face to face, if possible. You have to help the subcontractors to clear these hurdles. Subcontractors' issues are your issues.

Again, all the status reports from the subcontractors should be dated, documented, and stored in their specific folders.

As the project manager, you have to arrange the weekly, monthly, or as required, upper management project status reports and present them to upper management in meetings. These upper management project status reports should cover project schedule and cost performance indices for each task group, risk and problem assessment, scope change assessment, good news and bad news regarding the project, customers, subcontractors, and regulatory agencies.

If there is an important project issue or a risk management situation, an upper management meeting should be held immediately without waiting for the project status meeting. You should always go to the meeting with proposed solutions to risky issues. You should prepare cost-risk-benefit analyses of the alternative solutions. The presentations should be short in executive summary format. If an upper manager needs more details, he or she will ask for it. You can always see him or her separately to fill in the details.

You should always listen to upper management's suggestions during the project status meetings. If you do not like where they are going with a suggestion, do not oppose them in the meeting. Tell them that you would like to gather more facts and meet with them again. Do your homework and gather detailed facts. Show the upper manager who suggested the alternate approach, one-on-one before the meeting, that his or her solution is more risky and costly than the one you are proposing. Get his or her buy-in and then go to the general upper management meeting. If upper management still goes along with the more risky and costly approach, be firm and tell them that it is their decision and you will not take any responsibility for the consequences. Also, do not forget to summarize the confrontational event in the minutes of the meeting.

Here are some examples of upper management decisions that might hurt your project. There might be a subcontractor favored by upper management that you think is a risk. Upper management can make a decision to give priority to another project in manufacturing and push your project back. The effects of these decisions should be recorded so that everyone understands the consequences. Upper management might decide to authorize overtime work to finish your project even if it costs more. Its object is to ship the product as soon as possible so that reduced cash flow can be remedied. They can pull these kinds of gimmicks because they are looking at the overall picture. However, as an engineering project manager, you should record these decisions that adversely affect your project.

Periodic status reports should be a summary of the project at that point in time. Status reports should not go into every minor issue and alarm the customer or upper management. The reports should be concise and honest. You should expect similar status reports from your subcontractors.

Confidentiality and Intellectual Property

During the execution of a project, confidentiality and intellectual property requirements will need careful observation and compliance at the domestic and international project sites and at the subcontractor's. As the project manager, you have to know the confidentiality agreements and the IP rules covering your project and execute them to the letter of the contract during the whole duration of the project.

Also, you have to know your company's guidelines regarding confidentiality and IP protection procedures. You have to be on top of your company competitive standing in worldwide markets. If you do not understand the legal jargon in the project contract or confidentiality agreements, go to the company lawyer specializing in them and ask him or her to explain the IP rules and confidentiality agreements of the contract in layman's language. Do not try to figure out the solutions to complicated IP and confidentiality cases. If your company does not have an IP- and confidentiality-trained lawyer, go to a recommended one outside your company.

Some customers are very particular about confidentiality. They want their equipment built in an isolated area of the facility and not shown to anybody else. These cases occur in highly advanced technology and competitive edge equipment or component manufacturing. For example: If you are an original equipment manufacturer (OEM) to supply head stack assemblies to disk-drive companies who are competing fiercely for market share and technology advances by the hour, you have to assemble and test each customer's product in a separate production line and cannot show one customer's product to another.

In some confidential projects, the customer will require a separate and 100 percent dedicated team for their project. These team members cannot share any technical information regarding the project with others in your company. All the documents are checked out and in daily from document control, and no copies of these documents can be made or left sitting on desks in the offices. The customer has a right to audit your domestic and international project sites and your subcontractors anytime and unannounced.

For example, if a chip manufacturer is getting an advanced state-of-the-art ion milling machine built in your facility, they will ask you to isolate the ion mill assembly area and not show it to anyone else.

Inventions made by your company during the design and manufacturing of customer's product can be the property of your company. On the other hand, any invention based on mainly the customer's technical inputs during the design and manufacturing of the customer's product can be the property of the customer, and you have to notify the customer promptly regarding a new invention. Also, your company can be responsible for any infringements on patent rights, trade marks, designs, etc., caused by the design, manufacture, processing, testing, and sale of products similar to your customer's product.

Especially in international projects, IP protection and confidentiality can become very complicated and expensive. You have to know the patents issued in the design and manufacturing of your product in the countries that are involved with your project. Also, you want to protect your IP in the worldwide design and manufacturing centers of your product. For example, if you have a new invention in disk-drive technology, you want it patented both in the United States and Japan.

You have to make sure that your project team members, both domestic and international, are cognizant of the project IP and confidentiality rules. You have to make sure that they are keeping appropriate documentation for their new inventions. Sometimes, your customer might ask you to have very specific rules regarding need-to-know basis, document protection, security for their products, keeping their IP away from your other customer's competition, etc.

Good examples of these IP and confidentiality rules can be seen in the fast-paced computer industry. For example, in the design of magnetic recording heads for new disk drives, you have to keep the new drives' specifications, such as linear bit density, track density, and other unique features, customer specific and confidential. You have to be very careful during discussions with your customer's competitors, conference presentations, etc., so as not to make any slips regarding your customer's technical specifications, manufacturing timelines, yields, etc. During your test demonstrations for your customer, another competing customer might be next door in a conference room. You have to keep the two customers away from each other.

If you are manufacturing for your customer using the customer's specific and superior tooling, you cannot show that tooling to any of your other customers. Your customer might ask that manufacturing areas be isolated by curtains, walls, etc., for its product.

You have to pass on the same rules for IP protection and confidentiality down to your major subcontractors. You have to get them audited to make sure that they are following the IP protection and confidentiality rules because you are responsible for their actions.

In some projects, you have to enter the playing field without any IP protection or confidentiality agreements. In such cases, your primary goal is to protect your company.

For example, during negotiations with several automotive companies, who are your competitors, for joint manufacturing and testing of a new and an advanced state-of-the-art car engine, you have to bring out the aces of your design without revealing them in detail and giving away all the key elements, but again you have to convince your competitors that you have a superior design. You have to prepare well for the negotiations. You have to open the doors to your new and superior engine design, but you do not give them the keys, i.e., critical assumptions, critical calculations, critical tolerances, critical materials, etc. Also, you do not reveal the names of your key designers. In this particular car engine design project, the negotiations lasted several months, but no agreement was made between the competitors. However, the design company kept the key aspects of their advanced car engine protected.

In a different project in the computer disk-drive magnetic head technology, a $35 million advanced technology transfer agreement was made with a Japanese company. The technology transfer was only for a portion of the company's IP. The project manager for the project had to be very diligent not to provide any IP outside the agreement. Four Japanese engineers came to the company's U.S. production facilities for a year to learn the technology that was being transferred. The company engineering offices, production areas, test laboratories, etc., that the resident Japanese engineers could go to had to be defined and other areas restricted. Similar issues arose with the company employees. All the company employees had to be trained so that they could properly respond to the Japanese engineers' inquiries and questions and avoid discussing other companies IPs with them. This was a very tricky project in a fast-paced and highly competitive computer industry. The answer was in a very detailed project execution plan and in continuous training of all the company employees in order to keep the IP confidentiality awareness level up all the time.

While complying with all the project-related details and your company's confidentiality and IP rules during the execution of a project, you have to encourage your team members, both domestic and international, to record their new ideas and findings in engineering books and get them signed and dated by a colleague so that their new ideas and findings can be filed for a new patent.

Risk Management

Risk management is one of the most critical functions for a project manager during an international project execution. Identifying risks gets much tougher in an international project. Identifying risks is an engineering project management art backed by experience, gut feeling, listening, good monitoring of every task, good monitoring of every subcontractor, and not ignoring any negative signs. Small and ignored negative signs might come back and bite you. Risky tasks can be identified by paying close attention to subcontractors' performances; project team members' performances; customers' teams performances; schedule delays; cost overruns; hidden and overlooked specifications; tight specifications; leading-edge technology specifications; surprises in design, manufacturing, testing, and yields; and scope change creeps. Risky areas can also be identified in productive and detailed design reviews meetings.

For example, an overlooked washer material specification caused it to coin over a slot when the bolt was torqued to its design value. The design was done by an experienced design engineer, but the designer took a risk and specified a lower grade and cheaper washer. The washer material hardness was not adequate and was also overlooked during the design review. The washer coining issue was identified by surprise during the acceptance tests by the customer. Everyone involved had to rush to get the washer hardness specification changed, purchase special hardened washers, and get them plated. Product acceptance and shipment were delayed by a week.

Another risk identification area is in previous designs with design errors that are not fully resolved. For example, in an earlier project, a pressure intensifier in a hydraulic circuit was clogging up after a short operation. The designer told the project manager that the situation was fixed after inserting a filter into the inlet of the intensifier. The designer used the same pressure intensifier with a filter in the new project, but the project manager should have taken action to get this intensifier design issue investigated more thoroughly. The filter fix was only a partial one. After several discussions with the intensifier supplier, the project manager learned that they had to also insert a flow restrictor into the inlet of the pressure intensifier to limit the flow rate and prevent clogging. Not being able to thoroughly investigate and identify this design error during a previous project caused unnecessary schedule delay and cost overrun.

In another example, overlooking the utility specifications in an international project caused several weeks of delay in volume production. The project was to install automated manufacturing assembly workstations in a Malaysian facility. The project team engineers and ultimately the project manager overlooked the available utility standards and how they would affect the operation of the automated manufacturing system. Everything was installed on time and operated beautifully for a week, but the voltage fluctuations and the power outages were creating unacceptable interruptions in production. The team had to rush to get uninterrupted power supplies and voltage regulators from the United States and install them into the power inlets of the automated equipment to remedy the situation. This risk should have been identified at the design phase of the project.

In another international project, customer's team members changed in the middle of the project and caused the following issue during equipment installation. The customer was responsible for laying out the power lines between the power supply and a solenoid-operated control panel. At the beginning of the project, voltage drop calculations were done and the maximum allowable power line sizes and lengths were determined. Unfortunately, a new team of customer's engineers who were doing the installation at the final installation site overlooked the maximum power line lengths and rerouted the power lines to make them more accessible. This change caused excessive voltage drops and therefore erratic behavior at the solenoid valves. The project manager should have warned the new customer's team about the voltage drop sensitivity of the control panel components. Also, the company's field engineers should have been thoroughly trained on critical system installation parameters.

Risky areas correlate well with inexperienced engineers. You have to get their work checked and reviewed in great detail. You can also make them work together with a seasoned engineer in a body system. A grooming body system for an inexperienced engineer will benefit the project and the new engineer, and also minimize the risks.

Risky areas correlate well with inexperienced international teams. You have to reinforce international teams with the correct dosage of experience and get them trained appropriately. You can design the best production tool in the world, but if you throw it over the wall into the hands of an inexperienced international team, the tool will fail.

Risky areas correlate well with overloaded engineers. Overloading engineers is a constant practice in industries. According to upper management's thinking, extra engineering work comes in free. All upper managers expect overtime engineering work without extra pay because engineers are highly paid professionals. However, there are perils hidden in this approach. You can ask an engineer to work overtime to finish a task that is in a crunch, but you have to give him or her time off or a reward after the task is completed. Engineers who work 60–80 hour a week constantly get burned out, their efficiency drops, and they become high risks to the project.

Risky areas correlate well with minimally controlled subcontractors. Even if the subcontractor has a good record and is a ship-to-stock type supplier, tight controls have to be applied to critical items for the project. Tight control starts with a detailed and binding purchase order contract that both sides agree on. As the project manager, you have to push your purchasing and vendor engineering departments to apply strict controls to minimize the risks coming from a subcontractor. Stiff penalties for late delivery, rewards for early delivery, periodic status meetings, no changes to specifications and acceptance procedures without written consent from the project manager, identifying the subcontractor project manager and other critical people who will work on the project, etc., are some of the items that should be detailed on the purchase order. As a project manager, you have to make sure that the subcontractor, your purchasing agent, and your vendor engineer understand all the critical parameters of the project.

Sometimes it is good to distribute the risk to different subcontractors instead of putting all the eggs in one basket. Cost-benefit analysis of the multisupplier approach should be made before such a decision is taken. If you are a large-enough company, you can bring a subcontractor's majority manufacturing capacity under your umbrella for a period. If you are a small company, your work gets shifted to the back burner. If you are a small company and using a particular subcontractor for the first and last time, risk management gets tougher. Also, if you are a small company and your subcontractor is a large one, risk management gets tougher. Small accounts always get lower priority. The only way to manage such a subcontractor is by applying very tight and firm control procedures.

There are many ways cost overruns can bite a project manager. The best way to avoid them is to complete a project on time. As the project lingers on, you see efficiency drop and more charges starting to infiltrate into your project's charge numbers. This happens, especially, if the company is in a down mode and the work is slow. People tend to charge to an active account to show that they are keeping busy. At this point, close out the charge numbers that are not needed and do not allow anyone to charge to your project without your approval.

Another reason for cost overruns can be the learning curve or the training needed for an engineer. If an engineer is using FEM for the first time in your project, make sure that a just amount of his or her time is charged to the company's general training account and not your project. This type of learning curve and training efficiency issues happen all the time. A good project team balanced between experienced and new engineers will solve this issue. Also, a tight separation of training charges versus the actual project charges would result in just costing to the project.

Your company can go into a project accepting a customer specification that is not achievable. You do your best design, but your tests show that you cannot meet some specification limits. For example, this happened many times in off-track bit error rate performance in disk drives. As the track densities increased, it became tougher and tougher to meet the off-track bit error rates in the magnetic recording heads that were designed for a particular drive. This risky area in specifications can be resolved by negotiating the specification limits with the customer. You should prepare the qualification heads test result distributions for off-track bit error rate, and negotiate face to face with your customer and agree on a fair and compromised specification limits that will give you decent yields and also allow the customer's drive to operate in a highly reliable bit error rate regime. You should not kill your back and your project team over an extremely tight specification. You should always go to your customer and negotiate a win–win solution.

Risky areas correlate well with a weak and an uncoordinated customer's team. If a customer's team is weak, and if they forgot to put in some critical items into their specifications, they will come to the project manager during the execution of the project and try to impose new and unattainable requirements. As an example, an automated system was designed just to pass a specified-size chain through.

During the kickoff meeting, the customer was asked if it was planning to pass through other items such as connectors through this system. The answer was no. Then, in the middle of the project, the customer came and said that it forgot to specify the chain link that had to pass through the system. The whole design had to be changed. At least this was a valid scope change that affected the project delivery and cost. As the project manager, you have to be proactive and manage the customer's team. If you see anything unusual in the customer's specifications or applied standards, go back to your customer and raise the question. An uncoordinated customer's team can also bring trouble and risk to a project.

Another area that is often overlooked and is a high-risk factor in an international project is shipping. Shipping costs, shipping times, shipping insurance, shipping damages, shipping logistics, packaging, customs, and freight forwarders are very crucial elements of international shipping. Even the special wood that has to be used in your packaging might have been specified by the regulations of the country that you are dealing with. The project manager has to make sure that all project-related shipping issues are covered by competent shipping companies and people and there is no room for surprises. When you package and ship your finished product, damage to it can be devastating to your project and customer. Heavy protection of gauges and electrical consoles for shipment is one of the good practices. Design and shock testing of appropriate shipping containers are a must. Shock, humidity, temperature variations, electrostatic damages, contamination, and water submersion damages during shipment can render a finished product unusable.

The bottom line is that you should not ignore any risky area of the project. A risky area does not remedy by itself. You should not procrastinate on decision making when a risky area pops up. If you smell the slightest smoke, go take action and put the fire out. Do not let it spread and burn down the whole project.

Fire Fighting

During a project execution, fire fighting always occurs. A lot of fire fighting can mean an inexperienced project manager, an inexperienced or short-handed project team, inadequate planning and scheduling, inadequate risk management, sub-par subcontractors, inappropriate company procedures, and weak company departments. There will always be some fire fighting. As the project manager, you should cultivate lessons learned from fire fighting, take corrective actions, and correct the risky areas with sound planning and intense follow through so that emergencies do not occur frequently. During the execution of a project, excessive fire fighting reduces the team's morale and puts the team's performance into a downward spiral.

For example, a weakness in the company's purchasing department caused the following fire fighting. A subcontractor was losing money while trying to comply with tight welding specifications and welding qualification procedures. The subcontractor wanted additional funds for the welding qualification expenses and was holding the finished critical component shipments as hostage. The purchasing agent did not inform the project manager in time while this impasse was brewing. The negotiations with the subcontractor started face-to-face at the last minute. It was difficult to bring the situation to a just solution. The company and therefore the project lost money on the final deal. Leaving the conflict to the last minute gave an upper hand to the subcontractor, required a speedy resolution, and caused delays in the project. The purchasing agent should have checked the status of the subcontractor a couple of times a week and given a full report to the project manager without any delay.

In another example, inappropriate company procedures for tracing raw material lots through its manufacturing processes caused a lot of headaches during the execution of a project. The traceability of a material heat lot from a steel mill throughout its manufacturing and usage life was required in a project contract. During the final inspection of the product, the customer's inspector saw that there was no heat lot number stamped on some of the steel pieces. They were stamped originally but machined off during intermediate operations. The whole manufacturing and quality group scrambled to trace back each manufactured component and find the missing material heat lot numbers. You as the project manager had to make sure that a foolproof traceability system was in place at the beginning of the project to meet the project contract requirements, namely, that the steel heat lot number should not have disappeared after machining operations and after painting. When a failure occurs in the field or when the customer inspects your product, you should be able to trace all the manufactured components to their material certificates, and you should not have to scramble to determine them.

Another fire fighting example relates to the shelf life of photoresist in wafer fabrication. Every time there was an issue with the photolithography process, all engineers scrambled to find out the cause by sifting through hundreds of possible variables. One of the culprits was usage of out-of-date photoresist in the photolithography process. Out-of-date photoresist usage occurred at least once a month. A simple and a foolproof shelf-life expiration date system will eliminate one of the variables during fire fighting. If your photolithography operation goes out of control, you should not suspect the expiration date of that lot anytime. You do not have to run around and find out what lots are received when and what their working life expiration dates are.

If an issue keeps coming up and causes fire fighting all the time, then the solution to this issue is not permanent one. It is temporary, and you should be assured that it will come back to bite you again and again. You better gather everyone involved and devise a permanent solution to the problem. You have to also encourage the international project sites to find permanent solutions to an issue and not live with patchy ones.

Another wafer fabrication fire fighting example was from a deposition process that was going out of control for deposition thickness. The process team struggled to bring it under control, and after a couple of runs, it went out of control again.

It might be that the equipment was old or the specifications were too tight for the aged process equipment. It might have been caused by some gremlin that no one could figure out in a rush. The only way to solve the issue was to stop fire fighting and assign a special team that analyzed all the causes and effects in order to bring a lasting solution to the deposition thickness issue. A controlled and a detailed cause and effect analysis that lasted five days found the problem in the out-of-flat wafer-holding fixture.

Especially in offshore operations, fire fighting is unfortunately the norm because of inexperience and cost and time pressures. A good engineering project manager trains and motivates offshore engineers to go after permanent solutions. A good engineering project manager fights hard and convinces upper management to get extra funding, training, and manpower to design in enhancements into the systems to eliminate major fire fighting issues in offshore operations. In a Pareto chart of fire fighting issues, if you can find permanent solutions to 90 percent of the issues that occur during the execution of a project, then you would be doing an excellent job of stabilizing the project executions and your team's morale.

Most stressful fire fighting occurs in short-handed project teams. Constantly changing team members' tasks, delaying some tasks to meet upcoming milestones, shifting priorities to fill in the gaps, etc., bring in chaos to the execution of a project. This type of a constant fire fighting mode increases the stress levels fast and degrades the team's performance. In such cases the project manager has to meet with upper management immediately and request the necessary forces. These reinforcements to the team can come from internal sources, from consultants, from subcontractors, or from other companies.

A good example of short-handed fire fighting occurred during training for and installation of a system on an offshore oil platform in the North Sea. An inexperienced project manager assigned a new hydraulics engineer, who had never been offshore, to take on these demanding tasks. The new engineer went through and completed his offshore safety training courses and appeared to be ready for the challenge. After several weeks of working in freezing temperatures and teleconferencing daily with the project manager to get technical help, the project was not gaining any ground at all. The customer was very edgy and losing patience. The project manager went to upper management, threw his hands up, and asked for immediate help. At this time, there was an experienced offshore field engineer who quit the company and was sailing around the world. Human resources was able to locate him in Tahiti, and together, they and the project manager were able to convince the experienced field engineer to abandon his adventure and travel to the North Sea as a handsomely paid consultant for a month.

Fire fighting during the execution of an international project will transform a project manager into a seasoned professional. He or she will not fall into similar traps, will not make similar errors, and will take proactive actions to minimize fire fighting in future projects.

Adapting to Change

As the project manager, you have to maneuver your project team and your company to adapt to change during the execution of a project. Changes in a project can come from many sources such as scope, specifications, customer's personnel, upper management, team members, subcontractors, and technology. During a project's execution, change is inevitable. You have to smooth out the instabilities and the ripple effects that are caused by change.

Project scope changes have to be analyzed very carefully to assess the domestic and international teams' personnel impact, cost impact, and schedule impact. Sometimes it is a better practice to keep the major project scope changes separate from the original contract and generate a new project contract. Amending the whole contract for a major scope change might push out the milestone payments, affect the completion of ongoing tasks, and hurt your company in liquidated damages.

Minor project scope changes can be done without a formal contract modification but always by a written understanding between two project managers. A formal contract modification might unduly cost the companies time and money. A typical engineering change order (ECO) proposal and authorization trail for an international project, starting with the project manager and going through a maze of steps, is given in Figure 5.1.

A minor ECO process might take one to two weeks to complete, and involve a couple of authorizations during the approval process. A major ECO process might take a couple of months to complete, and involve a couple of dozen of authorizations during the approval process.

Specification changes can be proposed by your customer, team, or subcontractors. All specification changes should be analyzed from form, fit, and function of the product and from their impact on cost and schedule. A simple specification change might mean a huge change in scope. All specification changes should be approved by you and documented in the design basis. Specification clarifications should be treated the same way. No gray areas or words should be left to interpretation by others.

For example, a "smooth surface" callout on a specification is meaningless. The numerical value for the "smooth surface" along with its measurement method should be specified. Also, some projects start with specifications that are full of TBDs (to be determined later bombs). If such callouts are not clarified at the beginning of a project, it will be difficult to adopt clarifications for these TBDs during the execution phase of the project.

Other kinds of specification changes that degrade the quality of a product in a project are add-ons. This type of product degradation is experienced in software developments. The customer requests for add-ons keep coming during the development of the software. Time and funding restraints cause the final product to be patchy and difficult to debug.

1. Project Manager fills out the project change order proposal and authorization form (ECO form)

   + Define the scope of the ECO

   + Define tasks, manpower required, schedule, milestones

   + Create ECO cost model

   + Assess intellectual property

   + Assess effects of this ECO on the main project

   + Discuss and update ECO with customer's project manager

   + Discuss and update ECO with company's sales manager

   + Discuss and update ECO with your supervisor

   + Discuss final ECO with the project team (only involved members)

   + Iterate on discussions until a final version is reached

2. Obtain company's ECO approval signatures

3. Send the ECO form to the company sales manager

4. Sales manager obtains the customer's project manager approval signature in San Jose, California

5. Sales manager obtains the customer's purchasing department approval signatures in Germany

6. Customer's purchasing department in Germany amends the project purchase order and sends it to the sales manager

7. Sales manager sends a copy of the amended purchase order to the project manager and to the company's contracts department

8. Contracts department modifies the project cost model

9. Project manager updates the specifications summary, the cost and the schedule indices, and is authorized to start the tasks defined by the ECO

Figure 5.1　Engineering change order (ECO) and authorization trail for an international project.

During the course of the project, there can be changes in the customer's interface personnel. You should train the new personnel on the history of the project. You should support your training statements with dated documents and gain immediate trust of the new personnel. They will come to you with all kinds of questions and clarifications because you are the person who knows the project inside out.

During the course of the project, there can be changes in your upper management. You have to train the new management on the history of the project. You have to brief them on the plusses and the minuses of the project. You have to gain their trust and commitment to back you up in your requests and decisions.

During the execution of the project, your team members, both domestically and internationally, might change. This causes the most instability in a project, especially if the change affects a prominent member of the project team. A team member might quit, even worse, might jump ship and go to your competitor, might wed, take maternity leave, might get injured or sick, etc. You have to deal with all these instabilities and keep the team motivation up and the team unification tight.

Adapting to personnel change at international project sites can be more demanding. The international project site might need support people who can be sent to the international project site immediately. The international project site's new members might need extensive training. As the project manager, you have to smooth out these interruptions and get all tasks on track as fast as you can.

For example, your software engineer leaves the company unexpectedly. He is close to completing the coding for his task. The replacement software engineer has to learn the program specifications. He might patch up the incomplete program and finish it, but this approach might be risky. He might start to write the code from scratch using his own style, and this approach might lengthen the task duration. You have to work very closely with the new software engineer and try to get the transition to be as smooth as possible. You have to bring unity between the new engineer and the other engineers who are involved in completion of this task, such as code testing, system integration, etc.

Handing over a task from one task owner to a new one in the middle always causes a setback. The deeper the team member is into his or her task, the bigger the setback is. One of the ways to minimize the handover setback is to make the new task assignee work together at least a month in tandem with the person leaving. Another way is to devote the final couple of weeks of the leaving team member to document extensively what has been done. This documenting should be done under strict supervision. Otherwise, the quality of task documenting tends to be weak, especially if the task owner is leaving the company under adverse conditions.

During the execution of a project, subcontractor changes can cause major ripple effects depending upon how major the subcontractor is and what delays will be encountered by going with a replacement. You have to train the new subcontractor team and give it a smooth jumpstart. The reasons for subcontractor change can vary a lot. The subcontractor might be bought out or might go bankrupt. The subcontractor's new president might not like your company's president; let us say there might be an engrained animosity between the two. The subcontractor might fail to perform. Your project's project manager at the subcontractor's might quit.

A Japanese subcontractor was a sole source supplier of sliders for a head stack assembly company that supplied completed head stack assemblies to a major computer disk-drive company. The subcontractors and the contractor went through a tedious qualification process, and volume production of disk drives at the customer was in full swing. The Japanese subcontractor announced that it was quitting slider manufacturing operations in three months. This was quite a challenge to the manufacturing process. A new slider subcontractor had to be found with sufficient capacities, and the new subcontractors sliders, and the head stack assemblies with these new sliders, had to be re-qualified. The project manager for the head stack assembly company and the customer's project manager got together and devised a very detailed plan to get qualifications completed in the next three months by considering all the risk factors. Such a major change can affect a company's revenues substantially and cause layoffs if the change is not dealt with effectively in time.

It gets tricky to implement technology advances into your project in the middle of project execution. Delays due to learning curve, issues that pop up in immature new technologies, or budget issues can hurt the project. There can be also cases where new technologies will help speed up your project.

For example, in a project the customer started to use laser measurement techniques for its structural interface measurements. The equipment manufacturer was still using assembly techniques utilizing machined templates for its equipment. Laser measurements for structural interface between the manufacturer's equipment and the customer's structural envelope were an order of magnitude more accurate and provided advantages during installation. You, as the project manager, have to adopt this improved measurement technique as soon as possible. Your measurement techniques should be at least as good as your customer's so that you can achieve good correlation and have an uneventful installation.

In another example, you are measuring fluid contamination using visual samples under a microscope by comparing them to standard pictures. However, your customer has an in-line fluid flow sampling by pattern recognition. You have to urge your quality department to improve its measurement technique and be in line with the customer.

There can be also changes in a project due to natural disasters. For example, materials bought in Houston (Gulf of Mexico) were delayed two weeks due to hurricane Rita. The project manager formally asked the customer to add two weeks to the delivery schedule after thoroughly assessing the impact of material delay to the project's manufacturing schedule. He also looked at several alternatives such as overtime work or subcontracting to recover lost time. He gave the customer the option of extra overtime cost to finish the project on time or two more extra weeks for delivery.

We live in a constantly evolving world. You have to maneuver your project team and your company to adapt to change during the execution of a project.

The motto for the computer companies during the 1980s was automate, emigrate, or evaporate. Even these mottos evolve in time.

Controlling the Project

During the project execution phase, controlling the project means being on top of every one of its aspects. You have to control every team player, every task, and every metric for the international project in a virtual environment. Controlling is not by any means micromanaging a project. It means you know the status of every task, the personal motivation and status of each team member, the status of every subcontractor, your customer, and your upper management.

If a team member is getting married, he or she is going to take off two weeks, and you are not aware of this, then your project is in trouble. If your international division is going on a strike that might affect the project, and you are not on top of what is going on, then your project is in trouble. If your counterpart at the customer is planning to leave his or her job and you have not heard about this, then your project is in trouble.

You have to follow the schedule performance and cost performance metrics for each task group very closely. You have to verify, or get verified by a dependable team member in person, the progress being made at your international project sites and at your major subcontractor's. You have to take immediate risk management decisions and not procrastinate if you want to cross the finish line within schedule and within budget. Even if you do not meet the project metrics right on but inform upper management and your customer on time and take appropriate actions to remedy the situation, then you are in control of the project.

An example of controlling a cost overrun goes like this. Budget for ten sub-systems in a system project was $200,000, and $3,000,000 was the total project budget. By the time the project was realized and the subsystem design was completed, two years had passed, and the original budget estimate was obsolete. The subcontractor's cost for the ten subsystems came out to be $400,000 due to material cost increases and tight tolerances. Cost reduction efforts were launched by the project manager. By opening up manufacturing tolerances, relaxing material qualification requirements, working with the subcontractor closely to go over every requirement in the design drawings, the design team and the subcontractor were able to reduce the total cost of the ten subsystems by $40,000 to $360,000. Upper management was briefed on the situation, who allowed the cost savings from other subsystems to be transferred to the cost-overrun subsystem's budget. Also, there was no contingency fund allocation in the project. Every effort was made to complete the project on time in order not to accrue any additional expenses. The project finished on schedule, but with a 7 percent cost overrun.

There can be many situations that are outside your control where you cannot avoid a schedule slip or a cost overrun. All of a sudden, the price of steel can jump up and affect your project. You might have to purchase the required steel ahead of time and stock it to remedy a forecasted steel price increase. If you have a lot of international travel scheduled for the project, the increase in airline fares might bite you. You might have to curb the travel quantity and rely on teleconferencing or videoconferencing.

There can also be situations that you cannot control inside your company. You do not have the authority to straighten out the dynamics of other departments. The manufacturing department might slip from schedule, the purchasing department might be overloaded, or the quality department might own an outdated inspection equipment. You have to fight these issues with the managers of these departments, and if these issues are not resolved in a timely fashion, you have to elevate the issues to appropriate upper management.

In a system design and manufacturing project, a project was almost complete and ready for the customer's final acceptance testing. The customer came back and informed the project manager that the overall project was being pushed out by a year because they missed the favorable weather window for installation in Siberia. The customer wanted to delay the system final acceptance tests, too. This was a disaster for the project manager. The project was going to linger on, inefficiencies were going to creep in, and project charges were going to pile up. The project manager proposed to the customer that the milestones be finished as originally scheduled except on-site training and installation. After the system equipment were bought off, the project manager proposed to store them at his company's secure area until the customer needed them. This reasonable proposal was accepted by the customer, and the project was completed on time and within budget. Only the on-site training and installation budget was set aside to be spent the following year.

Controlling a project does not only evolve around schedule and budget; controlling human factors affecting your project is also very crucial. The stress levels of your domestic and international team members, subcontractors, customer, and upper management regarding your project have to be kept under control, as also their training needs.

Training

Training is also a very crucial element of project execution. Training of domestic and international team members, subcontractors, customers, and upper management in certain fields will be necessary during the execution of the project. Such training requirements should be a part of the project plan. Project training requirements should be shared with the trainee's supervisor and the human resources department. Project training requirements should go into the personal record of each team member.

Training can be done one-on-one, at company classes, Web classes, outside classes, at universities, outside seminars, conventions, etc. As the project manager, do not schedule a training session close to a project milestone. Milestone pressures take priority, and training always suffers. Schedule training sessions outside the company premises, if possible. Disruptions to a trainee are a norm during in-house training sessions.

Another type of training occurs during the execution of a project when you get stuck in a technology field or when you want to enhance your knowledge in a certain area. To get to the technological depth you feel you need, you might have to hire consultants or university professors, or get experts from other divisions of your company.

For example, if your project is to analyze the contaminations on a disk surface in a disk drive, you better know all the chemical analysis methods that can be applied to disk surfaces or get the right people to help you to obtain the depth you need in chemical analysis methods of disk surfaces. Another example might come up from a project specification in fracture toughness of materials that your team does not have depth in, such as the crack tip opening displacement theory in very low temperatures.

Another type of training occurs in foreign cultures. For example, in a computer company, all the engineers and upper management who dealt with Japanese customers face-to-face had to take a class in Japanese language and Japanese culture. Greetings, meeting manners, small-talk manners, dinner manners, etc., were taught. Such introductory language and cultural training helped in dealing with the Japanese customers.

Training in foreign countries might be more challenging. Language differences might be an issue. You have to get a good simultaneous translator during the training sessions or rely heavily on pictorial presentations. Another option is to get the training notes translated into the native language and give the notes in both languages to the people involved.

For example, in a high-volume production project with operations in Singapore, Malaysia, Korea, Japan, France, and the United States, everyone in the company had to be trained in statistical process controls (SPC). This international project required multilingual textbooks, training instructors, auditors. A whole SPC training system was established worldwide. This was a huge project by itself. It took almost two years to get more than 10,000 employees certified in SPC.

It is unfortunate that some engineers regard training time as relaxation time. If possible, make sure that all training courses are certified and the trainee gets an engineering society certificate or a course grade from an accredited university after completion.

Some companies do their training during lunch hours or after work hours. You have to make sure that your team members do not take this as an infringement of their personal times. You have to talk to them about this dilemma and make them understand that training is also good for their advancement and to deepen knowledge of the involved technology. It would be good to bring in free lunches or dinners during the odd-hour training sessions.

Another good practice for an engineering project manager is to create a technical information folder regarding the project. This project-related technical information folder can reside in your engineering department or in the company library. You and your team members can collect all the new technical papers, patents, and conference proceedings that are relevant to your project in this folder. A technology-sharing system like this can keep all your team members up to date on what is happening in the fields related to your project.

Time Off

Vacations, maternity leaves, medical emergencies, weddings, family emergencies, sabbatical leaves, holidays, etc., are a way of life in project execution. You have to plan, take action and get help, shift priorities and tasks, and talk some team members into delaying some time-off events to be able to deal with absences during project execution.

Everything starts at the top. As the project manager, you should not take time off from your responsibilities for the duration of the project. The project suffers major setbacks and you lose your touch even in a week. The person who steps into your shoes for a week or two cannot carry on like you without the depth of knowledge you have regarding the project and the nuances of a dynamic and an international project system.

If the project takes longer than a year, you should have an assistant project manager who can pitch in when you are off. As mentioned earlier, some projects have dual project managers, namely, one for business and one for technical matters. It is easier to take time off under these circumstances.

Similar time-off ground rules should apply to the project team members. For example, if the project is delayed and it is critical acceptance test time, do not let the design engineer go on his or her prescheduled vacation or holiday. Ask him or her to delay the vacation and holiday. Dealing with vacation and holiday issues might be sticky when the team member has been away in a foreign country many weeks and is scheduled to come home for Thanksgiving or Christmas. The project should cover his or her losses and also give him or her some token, i.e., an extra-day vacation time or couple of show tickets, of appreciation for the personal sacrifice.

Also, when a team member is off for whatever reason, you have to cover his tracks and his action items that are due. You should get his or her password for the computer so that you can access, for example, a critical calculation that he or she is doing that might be needed, or a portion of the software that he or she is writing might be necessary meanwhile.

For example, when a test engineer went to Australia for honeymoon for three weeks, the test scripts he wrote for a project on his computer were a bear to locate during his absence. The test scripts were not complete, and they were not released into document control, but they became urgently needed to test a subsystem assembly for the project.

As the project manager, you should be cognizant of all the time-offs at the international project sites. Discuss time-off cases with the project leader of the international site at every communication. Similarly, you should be cognizant of the time-offs of your contacts at your customer's. When you send an e-mail message to your customer and by surprise you get an out-of-office message back for three weeks, you are not in control of your project. The same goes for your critical subcontractors. You should know all the planned time-offs that affect your project.

During the execution of the project, you as the leader have to perform all the functions mentioned in this chapter to perfection without burning yourself out. You might have to get reliable help in executing some of these functions. Overall, you have the ultimate responsibility to execute the project on schedule, within budget, and with satisfied customers, subcontractors, upper management, and, above all, satisfied and proud team members with a sense of accomplishment.

Checklist for Chapter 5

Team Composition

- Are you leading everyone involved with the project?
- Are you leading the domestic team members?
- Are you leading the international team members?
- Are you leading the team's contractors?
- Are you leading the customers' teams for the project?
- Are you leading the critical subcontractors' teams for the project?
- Are you leading the regulatory agencies' team for the project?
- Are you on top of every issue related to the project?

Team Management

- How much support do you have to provide to your international project sites?
- How often are you having virtual meetings with your international sites' project leaders?
- Do you need to have one-on-one virtual meetings with each member of the international project sites?
- How often are you having face-to-face meetings with your international project sites?
- Are you having one-on-one meetings with your domestic team members?
- What is the frequency of one-on-one meetings with each member of your domestic team?
- Are you holding the one-on-one meetings with each member of your domestic team at their offices?
- Are you having one-on-one meetings with your outside consultants and contractors?
- What is the frequency of one-on-one meetings with each consultant and contractor?
- How often are the domestic team meetings?
- Are you able to tie in your international project sites to your domestic team meetings?

- If you cannot tie in your international project sites to your domestic team meetings, are you having a virtual team meeting with each international site on the same day as your domestic team meeting?
- Does every project team member see you as a problem solver and a helper?
- Do you help every project team member in personal issues while keeping a respectable distance?
- Are you getting your team members trained about the customs and traditions of the countries you are dealing with?
- Are you acting as a pressure relief valve to your domestic and international teams?
- Are you responding immediately to questions and inquiries regarding the project from your domestic and international team members?
- How are you dealing with nonperforming team members?
- How are you dealing with team members who disrupt team harmony and team synergy?
- Are you bringing in the upper management and human resources department to resolve the team personnel issues?

Customer Management

- Do you know your customers' technical and nontechnical contacts regarding your project?
- Have you set up the communication guidelines between your domestic and international teams and the customers?
- What is your response time to the customers' requests and inquiries?
- What is your customers' response time to your requests and inquiries?
- Are you persistent and helping the customers get answers out of them?
- Are you getting all customer communication filed chronologically?
- Are you carefully evaluating all the scope-changes proposed by the customer?
- How are you dealing with the major scope changes? Are you cognizant of the whole scope-change procedure?
- How are you dealing with minor scope changes?
- Have you thought about how to deal with projects that are put on hold or canceled during the execution phase?
- How often do you have to submit project status reports to the customers?
- Are you following customers' standard formats for the status reports?
- Are you including solutions to the project issues in the status report after discussing and agreeing with customers' project managers?
- Are the project status reports going through your formal document control release process?
- Are you getting status reports from your customers during your periodic meetings regarding the overall project?

- Are you leading a well-organized preparation effort for your customers' visit to your domestic or international project teams' sites?
- Are you leading a well-organized preparation effort for your customers' visit to your domestic or international subcontractors' sites?
- If your customer's project team has a new project manager or a new team member, are you training him or her with regard to the history of the project?

Subcontractor Management

- Have you determined the level of control for each subcontractor, both domestic and international?
- Do you know the risk factors involving a critical subcontractor?
- Is there a chance that your subcontractor will bump your order when he gets a larger one?
- Are you monitoring the critical subcontractors and their critical subsuppliers very closely?
- Are you or your designate having periodic face-to-face meetings with your subcontractors?
- Are you or your designate going beyond the subcontractor's conference room and observing work in progress, raw materials, components, test equipment, quality control equipment, process control charts, and corrective action reports for your subproject?
- Do you have a detailed subproject plan from your subcontractor?
- Does your subcontractor know all the design or test requirements from regulatory agencies?
- Are the subcontractor's vacation times and plant shutdowns, and your vacation times and plant shutdowns, considered in the subproject plan?
- Does the subproject plan cover critical material and component receipt dates? Are there backup sources for these critical items?
- Is there a penalty clause in the subcontractor's purchase order agreement with respect to critical items receipt dates?
- Do you get a periodic subproject status report according to your company's status report format?
- Do you have to train your subcontractor?
- Do you have to help your subcontractor get ready for customers visits and for regulatory agency visits?
- Are you or your designate responding to questions and inquiries regarding the project from your subcontractors immediately?
- Are you or your designate treating your subcontractors as a part of your project team?
- Are you or your designate helping your subcontractors when they are in a bind?

Dealing with Upper Management

- Are you informing upper management about the status of your project regularly, i.e., at least monthly?
- Are you getting upper management's advice to solve the project's major issues?
- What is your response time to upper management's requests and inquiries?
- During the regular upper management status meetings, are you covering schedule and cost performance indices, good news about the project, project's major issues along with their solutions, upcoming milestones, and customer's overall project status?
- Are you informing upper management of international project sites about the status of your project regularly, i.e., at least monthly?
- If an upper manager cannot attend your status meeting, do you meet with him or her later for an overview of the project?
- Are you document controlling the status meeting minutes and distributing them to all involved upper managers?
- Are you having emergency upper management meetings regarding a major project issue if there is a quorum?
- Are you going into the emergency meetings with concise description of the issue at hand and with proposed solutions?
- If an upper manager cannot attend your emergency meeting, do you meet with him or her later for an overview of the issue and the decisions taken during the emergency meeting? Do not forget to listen to and consider his or her inputs regarding the issue at hand.
- Are you document controlling the emergency meeting minutes and distributing them to all involved upper managers?
- Are you inviting upper managers to important customer meetings, project team celebration meetings, patent certificate award meetings, and project ending meetings?
- Does an upper manager interfere with your project without first notifying you?
- Did you ask the upper manager who is interfering with your team's tasks to go first through you instead of directly going to your team members?
- Do any of the upper managers, domestic and international, give extra tasks to your team members behind your back?
- Did you ask the upper manager, domestic or international, who is giving extra tasks to your team members, to go first through you instead of directly going to your team members?

Regulatory Agency Management

- What are all the regulatory agencies' classification and certification requirements for the project?

- Do you know all of the contacts who will be dealing with your project at every regulatory agency?
- Do you know which subcontractors have to deal with the regulatory agencies and obtain design or test certificates for their products?
- What is your response time to regulatory agency requests and inquiries?
- What is the regulatory agency response time to your requests and inquiries?
- Do you know the details of the design packages that have to be prepared for each regulatory agency?
- Are you getting the design packages checked for completeness before they are submitted to regulatory agencies?
- Are you submitting only documents that have been released through your document control system?
- Do you know the details of the tests that have to be performed for regulatory agency certification?
- Are you getting all the test procedures checked for completeness?
- Do you know the testing houses who are authorized to perform certification tests especially in Europe or in other required countries?
- Are you checking your regulatory agencies periodically to see that they are on track in reviewing your design?
- Are you helping your regulatory agencies go through hurdles with ease while reviewing your design?
- Have you received all the required design or test certificates from your subcontractors?
- Are you entering all the design and test certificates into your document control?
- Are you sending copies of design and test certificates to your customers?

Surprises

- Generate fast solutions to surprises by taking actions yourself or as a team and by accurate planning.
- If finding a solution to a surprise is going to take time, inform the originator. Do not be silent and delay your response to the originator.
- If the surprise is critical and is affecting the project schedule and budget, immediately call an emergency upper management meeting, present your solutions, and get upper management's approval.
- If the surprise comes from a critical subcontractor, help him to find a solution.
- Inform your customer about the surprise after you determine the solution, and schedule and cost impacts.
- If the surprise is critical to your customers, meet with them face to face to discuss it along with the solution and schedule and cost impacts.

Errors

- Devise preventive ways and procedures to minimize errors.
- Pass on the knowledge of lessons learned from errors to all the team members.
- Do not reprimand a team member for an error made. Find a preventive solution together as a team so that similar errors do not occur again.
- Help your subcontractors minimize recurring errors. Propose corrective actions. Audit improvements.
- Take firm actions for recurring similar errors. These actions can vary from dismissing a team member to disqualifying a subcontractor.

Listening

- Listen to everyone, top to bottom, involved with your project. Encourage everyone to give inputs.
- Praise and reward people with constructive inputs.
- Listen to your customers' inputs.
- Listen to your subcontractors' inputs.
- Listen to regulatory agency inputs.
- Listen to inputs from people outside your project circle.
- Spread your image as being a good listener and an open-minded project manager regarding criticism.

Practical Solutions

- Be practical in choosing solutions to difficult issues.
- Brainstorm with your team to find practical solutions to an issue.
- Have effective design review meetings.
- Invite machinists, assemblers, and subcontractors who will deal with the design in your design review meeting.
- Eliminate tight tolerances from designs as much as you can.
- Groom your team members, especially novices, to be practical in finding solutions to issues.

Whatever It Takes

- Are you doing whatever it takes to complete a stalled task or an international deadlock on time and within budget without compromising your and your company's integrity?
- Have you brainstormed and considered all the options to solve an issue?

■ Do you have to go out of your project management responsibility boundaries and implement improvements in company procedures or improvements in other departments to complete a task successfully?

Meetings

■ Have you standardized meeting preparation, meeting management, and meeting minutes?
■ What are the document control procedures for meeting minutes?
■ Have you trained everyone on your domestic and international teams to follow the standardized meeting procedures?
■ Do you have distribution lists for different meeting minutes?
■ How do you call emergency meetings? Is everyone involved informed on time and appropriately?
■ How do you prevent inefficiencies in a meeting?
■ How do you control meetings with upper management?
■ Who is scribing the meeting minutes?
■ Do you need translators for the meeting?
■ Are the meeting time and the meeting initiation process clear to international participants?
■ Have you done a dry run before an important meeting, such as the design review meeting, with the customers?
■ Has every team member's responsibility for the upcoming important meeting seem defined clearly?
■ Are all the meeting presentation tools operational and complete?
■ Do not forget to bring a hand calculator and a unit conversion chart to the meeting.
■ Have you arranged food catering for the meeting?
■ What is the protocol for greetings, seating arrangements, opening remarks, etc., for the meeting?
■ Is the duration of the meeting comfortable for international participants with jet lag?
■ If the meeting is in another country or off site, have you chosen carefully from your team who the participants will be? Have you covered all the bases that might be discussed during this meeting?
■ Have you identified the team members who can lead important meetings according to the project meeting procedures during your absence?
■ Have you done a complete pre-test of your deliverables before the final acceptance test meeting with the customer and with the regulatory agency?
■ Do you have all the critical people on your team attending the final acceptance test meeting?
■ You should avoid having critical meetings during weekends and holidays.

- Are all the punch list items generated during the final acceptance test meeting within the scope of the project contract?
- If you fail the final acceptance testing, do not try to fix your deliverable in front of your customer.
- If the final acceptance test meeting is away from your home base, do you have the appropriate personnel, tools, and spare parts to run the tests at the remote test site?
- Cover project performance indices, tasks successes and failures, mistakes made, scope changes, upcoming important events, and important document additions to project folders during the project status meetings.
- Hold a project status meeting with your team members at least once a month and at most every two weeks in a year-long project.
- Task owners should present the status of their tasks during the project status meetings.
- Set up periodic project status meetings with your customers, subcontractors, and upper management.

Status Reports

- Status reports for your customers should be standardized, and should be controlled documents.
- In most projects, status reports to the customer should be monthly or bimonthly.
- Status reports to the customer should follow customer's preferred format.
- Status reports from your critical subcontractors should be standardized, and should be controlled documents.
- In most projects, status reports from subcontractors should be monthly or bimonthly.
- Status reports from subcontractors should follow your preferred format.
- A project status report for customers should at least cover: project issues and their solutions listed chronologically; updated project schedule; scope changes; action items owed to the customer by dates; action items owed by the customer by dates; major suppliers' issues; documents submitted to the customer for approval by date and by revision level; document comments received from the customer by date and by revision level; third-party design verification status.
- A project status report for customers should highlight the delinquent action items by the customer.
- Upper management project status reports should cover project schedule and cost performance indices, risk and problem assessment, scope change assessment, good news and bad news regarding the project, the customers' overall project status, major subcontractors' status, and regulatory agencies' status.

- You might have to push your customers to get things done at their end without antagonizing them.
- Project status reports should be a summary of the project events, and should not go into every minor detail of the project and create unnecessary excitement and discussions at the customers' or at the upper management level.

Confidentiality and Intellectual Property

- Do you know the IP rules and confidentiality agreement requirements covering your project?
- Do you know the IP rules and confidentiality requirements in your company?
- Do you have help from a lawyer to put the IP rules and confidentiality agreement requirements into layman's language?
- Did you relay the project's IP rules and confidentiality agreement requirements to your team members, domestic and international?
- Did you relay the project's IP rules and confidentiality agreement requirements to other departments dealing with your project?
- Did you relay the project's IP rules and confidentiality agreement requirements to your subcontractors?
- If you do not have any IP rules and confidentiality agreements in your contract, how are you going to protect your company's IP interests?
- Do your document control procedures comply with the customer's confidentiality requirements?
- Do your manufacturing and testing procedures comply with the customer's confidentiality requirements?
- Do you encourage your team members, both domestic and international, to jot down their new ideas and findings for patent applications?

Risk Management

- Have you identified the risky tasks in your project?
- Are you having detailed and productive design reviews?
- Are you encouraging your designers to eliminate tight tolerances?
- Are you negotiating with your customer to loosen up tight and impossible-to-manufacture tolerances from their specifications?
- Are you keeping a close watch on the leading-edge technology segments of your project?
- Are you constantly monitoring risky areas such as inexperienced engineers, overloaded engineers, critical subcontractors, and weak customer's teams?
- Are you supporting adequately your international project sites with experienced personnel?
- Are you taking immediate corrective actions to remedy a risky task?

- If a risky task starts to get out of hand, have you informed, and met with, your upper management with proposed solutions?
- Are you going to complete the project on time? How are the schedule performance indices looking? Are you monitoring them weekly?
- Are you getting constant inputs from your on-site vendor engineers for your critical subcontractors?
- Do you have competent and experienced people in charge of your international shipments?

Fire Fighting

- Are you taking corrective actions to minimize fire fighting?
- Is your project team's inexperience, domestic and international, causing the fire fighting?
- Is your team's short-handedness causing the fire fighting?
- Are your inadequate risk management procedures causing the fire fighting?
- Are some below-par company procedures causing the fire fighting?
- Are some weak company departments causing the fire fighting?
- Are your customers' constantly changing demands causing the fire fighting?
- Are your subcontractors' milestone slippages causing the fire fighting?
- Does a fire that keeps occurring over and over again need a permanent fix?
- Are you gathering everyone involved to devise a permanent solution to a recurring fire?
- If a recurring fire is companywide or in another department, are you getting upper management's involvement to remedy the situation permanently?
- Are you training and motivating your international team members to find permanent solutions to recurring fires?

Adapting to Change

- What are the personnel, cost, and schedule impact of changes in scope, specification, etc.?
- Is the change in scope, specification, etc., a major one? Does it need a formal contract modification?
- Do you know all the steps for a project change order authorization?
- Is the change in scope, specification, etc., a minor one? Can it be handled by a written understanding between the customer's project manager and yourself?
- How does the project specification change affect the form, fit, and function of your deliverables?
- You should take on the responsibility of training your customer's new personnel dealing with your project.

- You should take on the responsibility of training your upper management's new personnel regarding the history of your project.
- If there is a change in a project team member, domestic or international, plan a transition that is as smooth as possible.
- If the team member change creates a setback to your project, present the situation to your upper management with proposed solutions.
- If there is a change in your subcontractor, plan a transition that is as smooth as possible.
- If the subcontractor change creates a setback to your project, present the situation to your upper management with proposed solutions. Get upper management's nod before going to your customer.
- If the subcontractor change is a major one, discuss the situation face-to-face with the customer.
- Bring in technology changes into your project after doing a detailed risk and benefit analysis and discussing it with the customer.
- Changes caused by natural disasters should be worked out with the customer face-to-face to a mutually agreed-upon solution.
- Minimize the pressures resulting from a change on your project team members.

Controlling the Project

- Control every team player in your project.
- Control every task of your project.
- Do you know the motivation and stress level of every project team member?
- Do you know the status of every subcontractor?
- Do you know the status of your customers?
- Do you know the status of your upper management?
- Do you know the status of the required regulatory agency certifications?
- Control cost and schedule performance metrics for every task of your project. Review them at least weekly.
- Do not micromanage your project.
- Take quick and sound risk-management decisions.
- Bring project-related items, inside or outside your company that you cannot control, to the attention of your upper management immediately.

Training

- Do you have training plans for your domestic and international team members, subcontractors, customers, and upper management?
- Are these training plans included in your project schedule?
- Are you sharing every member's training requirement with his or her supervisor and with the human resources department?

- Are the project training requirements going into every team member's personal record?
- Do you have to train people in other languages?
- Are you avoiding training sessions close to a project milestone?
- Are you avoiding in-house training sessions?
- Are the training courses certified or accredited?
- Are the training hours being charged to the project or to the general company training cost buckets?
- Do you share project-related technical papers, patents, and conference proceedings with your team members?

Time Off

- Have you included scheduled time-offs into your project plan for every member of your project team, domestic and international?
- Have you included scheduled time-offs into your project plan for every member of your customers' project team?
- Have you included scheduled time-offs into your project plan for every member of your major subcontractors' project teams?
- A project manager should not take time off during the execution phase of a project unless it is a medical emergency or unless you have an assistant project manager or a dual project manager.
- For a long-duration project, get an assistant project manager or have dual project managers, namely, one for technical issues and one for business.
- Apply firm ground rules for time off for project team members. Discuss the time-off ground rules during the project kickoff meeting.
- Are you ready to cover the tracks of a team member when he or she takes time off?

Chapter 6

Closing an International Project

Very few international engineering projects come to a clean closure at the end of the projects. There can be scope extensions in your project. There can be several leftover deliverables that were not accepted by the customer during the initial acceptance tests, and these deliverables might be going through some revisions to satisfy the customer. The customer might not have reviewed and approved all project documents to "approved without comment" status. Some of the regulatory agency design or test certificates might not be complete. There can be installation and start-up issues at the overall project site. The overall project might be delayed, postponing your installation and start-up tasks. The customer might have lost interest in the project or shelved the project due to market pressures. If you have been designing a data communication module, your customer's competition might have come out with an improved module at an earlier time to market. The international standards covering the application of this data communication module might have shifted to your customer's competitive design.

The following project closure tasks that are a must for an international engineering project manager are meant for a project that is coming to a successful and clean conclusion. If for any reason the project lingers on, the project manager should complete the closure tasks that are feasible for that particular project.

For example, in one of the system design projects for offshore oil industry, the customer's project team was dismantled and reassigned to other projects as soon as all the system hardware was delivered. There was nobody left at the customer's team to give final review and approval to all the outstanding documents. It took the customer 18 months to reassign an engineer and get all the documents approved and released so that the final payment could be received and the project could be closed. Of course, the project engineer was also reassigned to other projects, but he had to spend about ten percent of his time for 18 months to close out this lingering project. During this period, the project engineer had to submit monthly project status reports and discuss with the customer on a weekly basis the delinquent action items.

After all the deliverables have been submitted to the customer and approved, there are several project closure tasks that a project manager has to complete. Some of the project closure tasks are preparing the final project status report for the customer; final project report for upper management with the final project metrics; reassigning the team members; having project completion luncheon, dinner or picnic; completing as-built drawings; getting final document approvals from the customer; closing out the project's contractors' contracts; archiving project files; releasing customer's or companies' equipment and materials that were used during the project; compiling a lessons-learned list and having meetings to explain lessons-learned items to all involved parties, including the major subcontractors and the customers; and the customers' evaluations of the project. Unfortunately, most of the time, a project manager is assigned to another project immediately after the project deliverables are completed, and does not finalize some of the closure tasks listed. This is a shortsighted approach in a company, and it gives rise to repeated errors and risks that could be prevented in future projects.

Final Status Reports

The final project status report for the customers should be after all the issues with the customer have been closed. For example, if there is an outstanding test certificate from a regulatory agency, or if there is a payment issue that has to be resolved, you cannot send a final status report to the customer. You have to keep the project open. The final project status report to the customer should state that it is the final status report and all items have been cleared and closed.

The final project status report to upper management should contain the final project schedule performance and cost performance metrics. You have to agree with the accounting department on the final cost figures of the project before your presentation to upper management. If there are still open tasks, payments, and receipts, you have to agree with the accounting department in a written form on final cost estimates so that you can prepare your final cost performance report. In addition, a list of lessons learned and suggestions for the areas of improvement in the company for future projects should be a part of the final status report for upper management. After the project deliverables have been completed and final payments from the customer have been received, the interest in a final report might fade away. It is advisable to keep the final status report to upper management short, concise, and to the point.

You have to receive all the final subproject status reports from your major sub-contractors. Your purchasing department should close out their contracts after your approval of the final status report. Also, your purchasing department should give subproject evaluations to your subcontractors with inputs from you and from other engineers who dealt with them during the project.

Other Project Closure Tasks

Once the project starts to phase out, you have to talk with every team member's supervisor, domestic and international, and understand what the future shows for each team member. You have to give every team member face-to-face project performance evaluations and provide input regarding these performance evaluations to the team members' supervisors and human resources departments. Some team members might go to a new project, some might get a promotion, some might move to a new department, some might be destined for a layoff, or some might be terminated. You as the project manager have to give your honest performance input to their supervisors and then he or she should discuss with the particular team member as to what comes next.

At the end of a successful project that had a good team effort, always complete the proceedings with a luncheon, dinner, or picnic, depending on your budget situation. Invite upper management, the customers' contacts, other departments that were involved with the project, the contractors, and the major subcontractors to this final event. At this event, recognize the achievers with certificates, plaques, team shirts, etc. Make sure that the highest upper manager that is present at the final event presents these mementos to their recipients.

Make sure that the project international sites also have similar project-ending get-togethers. If you can attend them, it will be quite a boost to their morale and commitment to future projects, and it will enhance their accomplishments in the just-concluded project.

During the rush of the final acceptance tests and deliverables, quite a few redlined drawings are done and as-built changes made to the product. You have to make sure that all the affected project drawings, software releases, installation and maintenance manuals, etc., are updated to reflect the final product that was delivered. This is one area most companies are relaxed about due to the rush to take on a new project or other priorities. Official as-built document updates always fall through the cracks. You as the project manager have to be diligent about these as-built updates and allocate manpower for them in your original project planning.

You have to receive the final reports, drawings, calculations, etc., from your contractors. You have to make sure that payments are made to them and their contracts closed out by your purchasing department.

You have to make sure that all the regulatory agencies' design and test certificates are complete, controlled documents and are submitted to the customers properly.

You have to archive all the project communication files through your information technology department. All electronic files should be read-only files, and nobody should be able to tamper with them. All paper files have to be filed in a known location in the company. All drawings, calculations, project documents, software programs, etc., should be in your document control, up to the latest revision levels. These latest revision level documents should match what the customer has in its document control for the project.

There might be several equipment or gauges or material that were used during your project that were consigned to you by your customer or borrowed from a subcontractor or from another division of your company. You have to make sure that all these consigned or borrowed items are sent back to their owners and that all paperwork is finalized.

Lessons Learned

Most people read history and learn from history to take the next step in life. It is the same concept in project management. Lessons learned from a project are precious for your progress as a project manager, for the progress of other project managers, and also for the improvement of your company. A compiled lessons-learned list should be broken up by the major subtasks of the project. In addition, the lessons-learned list within a subtask should be broken up into domestic and international project sites, customers, and major subcontractors divisions. You should call meetings with domestic and international upper managements to discuss the final project status report and all the items that are on the lessons-learned list. You should organize similar meetings with your domestic and international project team members. It is always good to have the lessons-learned team members' meetings after the upper management meetings so that you can relay to your team the improvements the company is planning to undertake as a result of the lessons-learned items.

The customers' portion of the lessons-learned items should be discussed with them. The major subcontractors' portion of the lessons-learned items particular to a subcontractor should be discussed with that particular subcontractor.

Customer's Project Evaluation

The key to a project's success is customer satisfaction. You as the international engineering project manager should do all you can to make your customer, external or internal, happy and proud of what you and your team have accomplished. Customer satisfaction can mean more and maybe bigger projects for your company and for you. Customer satisfaction words spread around fast in an industry. However, the opposite spreads around faster. A report card from the customer at the end of the project is a must. You have to give report cards to your subcontractors, too.

For example, after the completion of a data communication chip design project, it became very difficult to get a final project evaluation from the customer's project manager. He was always busy. He was thrown into managing other projects, and none of the persistent phone calls or e-mails were successful in getting him to complete the customer project evaluation form and return it. The project manager heard from his secretary that the customer's project manager was going to be at a technical conference the following week. The project manager made arrangements to attend the conference and caught up with him at the conference, and asked him to have coffee together for 15 minutes. The project manager asked the questions, filled out the form, and made the customer's project manager review, sign, and date the form to complete it on the spot. The project manager's determination got the job done, even if his coffee got cold.

Some companies have standard customer project evaluation forms with evaluation questions having satisfaction ratings, say, between 1 and 10. They send these forms to the customer's principals who were involved with the project and wait for a response. Most customers do not even bother to fill out such evaluation forms. This method is not an effective way of understanding what the customer's real gripes and real compliments are regarding a completed project. You as the project manager should pay a final visit to the customer and sit down with the customer's representatives for an hour and go over the whole project while identifying all the positive points and the negative points about the project execution. Record these points and make them a part of your final project status meeting with your upper management and with your team members. Your company should take action to remedy the weak points raised by the customer, and a copy of those actions should be sent to the customer as proof that your company and you are listening to the customer and always improving. These kinds of proactive actions also show your appreciation of the customer's constructive inputs and gives the customer a positive sign regarding your company for upcoming projects.

You should ask your customer one last question during the project evaluation meetings. Would you award my company another project like this one? You will hope that the answer is an unanimous "YES." Do not forget to take the customer's representatives out to lunch or dinner after this final project evaluation meeting.

The customers' project evaluation reports are also an evaluation of your international project management techniques. From the project lessons-learned list, your customers' inputs, subcontractors' inputs, upper managers' inputs, regulatory agencies' inputs, and finally, from your domestic and international team members' inputs, always improve your project management techniques, especially on international projects. You should always swear by the basic international project management principles but never stop enhancing your management techniques.

Checklist for Chapter 6

- Are all the issues regarding the project closed and approved by customers?
- Do you have a list of open items?
- What are the manpower, schedule, and cost estimates for the open items?
- Does the customer have the latest revision of all required drawings, calculations, and documents in his document control system?

Final Status Reports

- Prepare final project status report for the customers.
- Do you have the final cost estimates for the project? Have you agreed with your accounting department on the final project cost estimates?
- Prepare final status report for upper management including final project metrics.
- Did you meet with domestic and international upper managers to present the final project status report?
- Have you received final status reports from your major subcontractors?

Other Project Closure Tasks

- Are you helping in reassigning your team members?
- Have you completed each team member's, domestic and international, project performance evaluations?
- Have you discussed these project performance evaluations with each team member?
- Have you discussed these project performance evaluations with each team member's supervisor?
- Have you sent copies of these project performance evaluations to the human resources department?
- Are you having a project completion get-together with your domestic team?
- Are your international project sites having similar project completion get-togethers? Are you planning to attend them?
- Is your team completing the final as-built drawings and documents? Have you allocated manpower, time, and funds for as-built drawings and documents?
- Have you received all the necessary design and test certificates from the project's regulatory agencies?
- Have you closed out the subcontractors' contracts?
- Have you archived all the project files?
- Have you released company equipment used for the project?
- Have you released customer's equipment used for the project?

Lessons Learned

- Have you compiled a lessons-learned list by major subtasks?
- Have you presented the lessons-learned list to your domestic and international upper managers with proposed solutions?
- Have you presented the lessons-learned list to your domestic and international team members?
- Have you presented the pertinent lessons-learned list to your major subcontractors?
- Have you presented the pertinent lessons-learned list to your customers?

Customer's Project Evaluation

- Have you completed the customers' evaluations of the project with your customers during face-to-face meetings?
- Have you presented the customers' evaluation results to your domestic and international upper managers?
- Is your company taking action to remedy the weak segments of the company that you experienced during the execution of the project?
- Are you taking action to improve the weak areas of your international project management techniques that you experienced or received criticism for during the execution of the project?

Index